School Violence

Look for these and other books in the Lucent Overview Series:

Abortion
Acid Rain
Adoption
Advertising
AIDS
Alcoholism
Animal Rights
Artificial Organs
The Beginning of Writing
The Brain
Cancer
Censorship
Child Abuse
Children's Rights
Cities
The Collapse of the Soviet Union
Cults
Dealing with Death
Death Penalty
Democracy
Drug Abuse
Drugs and Sports
Drug Trafficking
Eating Disorders
Elections
Endangered Species
The End of Apartheid in South Africa
Energy Alternatives
Espionage
Ethnic Violence
Euthanasia
Extraterrestrial Life
Family Violence
Gangs
Garbage
Gay Rights
Genetic Engineering
The Greenhouse Effect
Gun Control
Hate Groups
Hazardous Waste
The Holocaust
Homeless Children

Homelessness
Illegal Immigration
Illiteracy
Immigration
Juvenile Crime
Medical Ethics
Memory
Mental Illness
Militias
Money
Ocean Pollution
Oil Spills
The Olympic Games
Organ Transplants
Ozone
The Palestinian-Israeli Accord
Pesticides
Police Brutality
Population
Poverty
Prisons
Rainforests
The Rebuilding of Bosnia
Recycling
The Reunification of Germany
Schools
Smoking
Space Exploration
Special Effects in the Movies
Sports in America
Suicide
Teen Alcoholism
Teen Pregnancy
The UFO Challenge
The United Nations
The U.S. Congress
The U.S. Presidency
Vanishing Wetlands
Vietnam
Women's Rights
World Hunger
Zoos

School Violence

by Jeff P. Jones

Lucent
Books

Library of Congress Cataloging-in-Publication Data

Jones, Jeffrey (Jeffrey P.)
    School violence / by Jeff P. Jones.
        p.   cm. — (Lucent overview series)
    Includes bibliographical references and index.
    ISBN 1-56006-710-1 (lib. bdg. : alk. paper)
    1. School violence—United States—Juvenile literature.
[1. School violence. 2. Violence.]   I. Title.   II. Series.
LB3013.3 .J67   2001
371.7'82'0973—dc21

00-010260

Contents

Introduction

A SCHOOL SHOULD BE a safe place, and, historically, schools in the United States have been relatively safe. Over the past decade, however, many people have begun to question the safety of American schools. Several mass killings at schools have focused the nation's attention on school safety. Although such extreme episodes are rare, students and teachers across the country are targets of threats and bullying every day.

In the early 1990s, a rash of high-profile school shootings raised concerns about school violence, and researchers began to study the issue more closely. They found that schools are generally safe but that violence between students does occur on campuses nationwide. Although school deaths are extremely rare, everyday school violence such as fistfights and bullying is more common. Each year, more than 3 million crimes are committed in or near public schools. The crimes range from theft, vandalism, and fights without a weapon to murder, rape, and attacks with a weapon.

Perhaps the most shocking discovery was that, even though school violence overall did not increase significantly during the 1990s, the fear of school violence among students and educators rose sharply. Researchers suggest that this heightened fear may be a result of the new dangers that students faced, including more guns, gangs, and drugs in schools.

Despite the increased fear and public alarm over school violence, there is little agreement about its causes. Many people blame a shift in young people's attitudes toward a lack of respect for life. Others claim that easy access to guns has raised the level of violence. A large number of parents and educators cite an increasingly violent media for changes in adolescent attitudes and behavior. Sociologists and others claim that deteriorated inner-city neighborhoods and a dramatic increase in gangs since the late 1980s are fueling school violence. And still others see the breakdown of the family and abusive homes as causes.

Even though all of these theories have been offered, many researchers warn against looking for one primary factor as the cause of school violence. "It is dangerous to take a very complex thing and whittle it down to one single cause," says Alan Leschied, a leading Canadian researcher on teen violence. "It is a combination of how culture is working, how the family is working, how the culture within [a] school [is] developing."[1]

Students console one another during an emotional prayer vigil for the shooting victims of Columbine High School.

8

Tragic consequences

Sometimes, the tragic consequences of school violence get lost amid the controversy. Families who have lost children to school violence are forever changed, and victims who survive may live in fear for the rest of their lives. More than a year after being shot in her high school cafeteria in Springfield, Oregon, by a fifteen-year-old classmate, one student named Jennifer was still dealing with the consequences. People stare at her scars when she wears a swimsuit, she says, and loud noises still startle her. When she confronted her attacker, Kip Kinkel, at his trial, she said,

> Until these scars go away, until my hand moves again, until I can look at my boyfriend and he doesn't feel guilty that he couldn't save his friend Mike [a student Kinkel killed], until that happens, you know the emotional effects won't go away.[2]

1

The Scope of School Violence

ALMOST EVERY WEEK a dramatic new incident of school violence grabs the nation's attention. Headlines such as "Boy, 6, Shoots, Kills Girl in Class: First-Graders May Have Quarreled," carried by the *San Diego Union-Tribune* in March 2000, seem to have become commonplace. Since the early 1990s, shootings at American schools have become big news stories not only with the national but also the international media.

The drama of these incidents—striking even at the lowest grades of elementary school—and the ensuing media coverage have made school safety a hot topic. Today, public concern for school violence is greater than ever. When President Clinton said, "The recent series of killings in our schools has seared the heart of America about as much as anything I can remember in a long, long time,"[3] on July 7, 1998, he spoke for many people.

High-profile school violence

Less than a year after President Clinton uttered that statement, the worst act of school violence in recent history took place at Columbine High School in Littleton, Colorado. Armed with assault guns and homemade bombs, two Columbine seniors attacked the school on April 20, 1999. As the gunmen made their way through the school, one student recalled, "They were shooting everywhere; it seemed like they wanted to kill everything in sight. I've never been

Columbine High School students run from their school after gunmen opened fire on terrified students.

so frightened in my life. It was run for your life or die."[4] The gunmen killed twelve students and one teacher and injured twenty-three others before shooting themselves. They fired off almost a thousand rounds. The killers, Eric Harris and Dylan Klebold, had been two months away from graduating high school. Both boys had played Little League sports as children and their parents had attended all their games, even their practices. They were described as "model employees" at the pizza parlor where they worked. The killing spree shocked the community—and nation—and left many more questions than answers.

The Columbine tragedy received massive media coverage, and people began to worry that such attacks might start happening everywhere. The understandable distress and fear that resulted in the wake of the terrible events at Columbine overshadow the fact that such premeditated attacks remain highly unusual. Vincent Schiraldi, director of the Justice Policy Institute (JPI), a nonprofit research group in Washington, D.C., says that students have less than a one-in-a-million chance of being killed at school: "Despite the increased attention the subject has been garnering, school shootings are extremely rare and are not on the increase."[5]

Everyday school violence

This does not mean that threats to personal safety at school do not exist. Far from it. In fact, the attention given to the Columbine tragedy and other high-profile school shootings often obscures a more common, related problem—that of everyday school violence. This type of violence ranges from hostile teasing, bullying, and fistfights to physical attacks with weapons, robbery, and even rape. This everyday problem is not as dramatic as gunmen attacking a school and does not make the news nearly as often. Nevertheless, everyday school violence is a problem that concerns students, parents, teachers, and administrators. Kara, a fifteen-year-old sophomore, described the everyday violence at her school: "You bump someone by accident, and they think you did it on purpose," she says. "They either shove you back, or they threaten to get you later."[6]

Violent crime at schools occurs less often than so-called nonviolent crime. Only about 8 percent (approximately 202,000) of the total crimes that occurred at schools in 1996–1997, for example, were considered serious or violent. A serious or violent crime includes rape, sexual assault, robbery, or fights with a weapon.

The most common form of nonviolent school crime is theft. Of the 2.7 million incidents reported in 1997, for example, 1.6 million were thefts. The most common form of violent school crime is fistfights (without weapons) between students. These are categorized as simple assaults and, in 1997, 853,400 were reported.

Everyday violence occurs at schools across the nation regardless of location, but it is a substantially bigger problem at large, inner-city schools. In 1998, the National Center for Education Statistics (NCES) conducted a survey of more than twelve hundred principals that measured the rates of violence and crime at their schools. The NCES study showed that inner-city schools experienced more violence than schools in nonurban settings. According to the study, 17 percent of urban schools reported at least one serious violent crime during the previous year, as compared with 8 percent of rural and 5 percent of suburban schools.

The victims of school violence

The student population at inner-city schools tends to be poor, ethnic minorities. Research shows that these young people are victims of school violence more often than their peers outside the inner city and that the violence in these areas often involves weapons. An article in the 1995 *Educational Psychology Review*, for example, reported that African American and Hispanic students at every grade level are more likely than whites to report being threatened with or injured by a weapon at school. Furthermore, in a study of ten inner-city public schools in California, Louisiana, New Jersey, and Illinois, two-thirds of the students reported that they personally knew someone who had been shot, stabbed, or otherwise assaulted at school.

When violence occurs on campus, regardless of the school's location, the victims have traditionally been male.

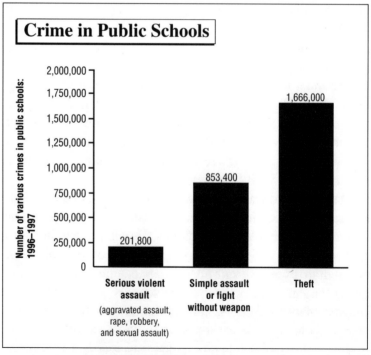

Crime in Public Schools

Number of various crimes in public schools: 1996–1997

Source: National Center for Education Statistics.

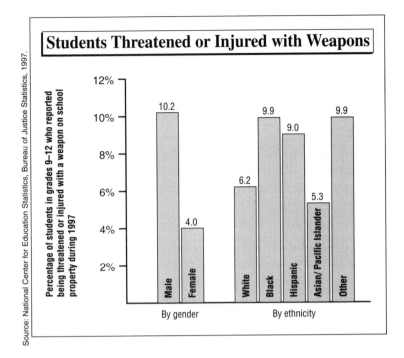

Students Threatened or Injured with Weapons

Percentage of students in grades 9–12 who reported being threatened or injured with a weapon on school property during 1997

By gender

Male 10.2
Female 4.0

By ethnicity

White 6.2
Black 9.9
Hispanic 9.0
Asian/ Pacific Islander 5.3
Other 9.9

In 1992, the Centers for Disease Control and Prevention reported that, nationally, half of all boys claimed to have been physically attacked by someone at school. More recently, however, female students have increasingly begun to fall victim to school violence. During the 1996–1997 school year, for the first time the largest number of deaths due to school violence were female students, many of which resulted from disputes involving jealous boyfriends. These statistics show that, although dramatic incidents of school violence are rare, everyday violence does affect many different types of students.

Though such statistics are helpful in understanding the scope of school violence, they do not provide a complete picture of the problem. Sometimes it is hard to say just how widespread the problem really is because school violence is very difficult to track. There is no standard, easy way to gather information on school violence; no single agency is responsible for collecting official statistics on the problem.

Further complicating the efforts to understand the severity and frequency of violence in schools is the fact that many incidents of school violence go unreported. When school officials are surveyed in studies like the one done by the NCES, principals sometimes downplay the amount of violence in their schools, perhaps to prevent harm to their school's reputation and a possible decrease in enrollment.

Another reason the problem often goes unreported is that students themselves rarely report school violence to authorities. They are often embarrassed or afraid they might get into trouble. A 1991 study found that only one in five victims of school violence reported the incident to police.

Teachers and school violence

Whereas students may fail to report school violence, teachers have become more vigilant than ever in reporting such incidents to the media and police. The high-profile school shootings during the 1990s heightened concerns about safety on school campuses across the country. "Teachers now report any mention of violence, even references in short stories, journal entries, notes passed between students and drawings of violent acts,"[7] writes school violence researcher Kathy Koch.

Their vigilance may be, in part, due to the fact that teachers themselves are increasingly becoming victims of violence. The 1999 NCES study showed that, from 1993 to 1997, teachers from all grade levels were victims of 657,000 violent crimes, including rape or sexual assault, robbery, and attacks with or without a weapon. During the 1993–1994 school year alone, the report stated, 12 percent (about 341,000) of all teachers were threatened with injury by a student, and 4 percent (about 119,000) were physically attacked.

Are schools part of a new wave of youth violence?

Some people believe that teachers who encounter violence are victims of an increasingly violent youth population and that a new wave of youth violence is storming across the country. They point to alarming statistics that show that juvenile crime and arrest rates soared in the early 1990s. Some even claim that schools are at the center of this storm of violence and point to studies like one done in 1995 by *USA Today* that indicated that neighborhoods around inner-city schools were more violent than other similar areas not close to schools.

Such studies led many people to assume that youth violence was directly related to school violence. Although the two do appear to be linked in some ways, research has not proven that increased juvenile crime translates into increased school violence. When youth violence began to increase during the late 1980s, media reports on school shootings also began to appear. People naturally assumed that both problems were increasing and evolving into a new epidemic of violence centered in the schools.

Schools are still safe

Despite the screaming headlines and alarming claims, however, studies show that school violence is not increasing. The levels of crime and victimization in schools have remained relatively stable since 1989. There is no wave of violence washing over U.S. schools. In fact, according to the Department of Education (DOE), the chance of becoming a victim of school violence changed very little between 1989 and 1995.

Similarly, students are not more likely to be killed in schools. Between 1992 and 1998, the number of school deaths actually decreased by about 27 percent. Some researchers contend that a student is twice as likely to be struck by lightning than to be killed at school. "Kids are safer in schools than they are anywhere else in America,"[8] says William Modzeleski, director of the DOE's Safe and Drug-Free Schools Program.

Furthermore, the large majority of schools don't experience any serious violent crime at all. Only a small percentage of schools report serious violent incidents occurring on their campuses. These figures show that most schools are safe from serious violent acts, and a large number of schools are remarkably safe. According to a 1998 NCES study, 90 percent of public schools in 1996–1997 reported no serious violent crime to police and 43 percent reported no crime at all.

A matter of perspective

Despite the statistics and the experts' claims about the safety of schools, it is commonly believed that school violence is increasing. Dramatic school shootings have increased concern among almost everyone involved in education—students, parents, teachers, and administrators. People no longer see schools as safe havens. They argue that school violence is one of the worst problems in America today.

Certainly, any violence on school grounds anywhere is a concern. No student should be subjected to harassment, threats, or violence in school, and for those who are, the experience is, no doubt, troubling. The fear of school shootings, however, surpasses the reality in most cases. "Across the nation," writes Margaret Hamburg, a youth violence researcher, "there is grave concern that our children are no longer as safe from intimidation, serious injury, or death as they once were while at school or on their way to or from school."[9] Even though the odds of being killed at school are less than one in a million, 71 percent of those polled by the *Wall Street Journal* in 1999 believed that the occurrence of a school shooting was likely at their school.

Studies such as the *Wall Street Journal*'s reveal that, whether or not it is justified, the *perception* that schools are unsafe definitely exists. Many students believe that they are likely to become victims of violence at school. The perception of violence is highest in urban schools. According to the *American Journal of Diseases of Children* in 1992, 15 percent of students at inner-city schools feared for their safety almost all the time. Similarly, a Harris poll of two thousand teenagers in 1998 found that one in three teens who lived in violent neighborhoods (and one in nine overall) skipped classes at times for fear of violence at school.

The fear of violence also increases the opportunities for more violence. When students feel that their safety is threatened, they may decide to start carrying a weapon to school.

If the student gets into a fight, the presence of the weapon increases the chances that someone will get seriously hurt.

Even though school violence is not increasing, studies suggest that the fear of school violence is. One way researchers judge this is by asking students if they avoid certain places at school because they consider those places unsafe. In 1995, 2.1 million students stayed away from places at school they perceived as violent. "While data show that the actual rate of victimization has declined or remained constant over recent years," a 1999 NCES study concludes, "students seem to feel less safe at school now than just a few years ago."[10]

Increased gang presence

The increased presence of gangs in schools may be one reason for this rise in students' fears and in the overall perception that school violence is increasing. During the same period that students began to fear more for their safety at school, the number of gangs in schools also rose. Gangs tend to bring violence to schools, thereby increasing the fear among students.

Unlike the fear of increased violence in schools, the fear of gang violence in schools is not one of perception. Schools with a strong gang presence do experience increased violence. In 1995, only 3 percent of students at schools without gangs were victims of violence, compared with the more than 7 percent of students who were victimized at schools with gangs.

The fear of school violence affects education

Whether brought in by gangs or not, violence and the fear of violence are widespread problems because they disrupt education. Young people who worry about violence or who are victims of violence cannot focus on their education. Regardless of whether a student's fear of violence is real or exaggerated, it often prevents learning.

Fear of violence also affects the entire school atmosphere. Students' attention spans have decreased, and some students are less eager to attend school because of the

Experts believe that an increased presence of gangs in schools may be responsible for the overall perception by Americans that school violence is on the rise.

threat of violence. Similarly, some teachers are less likely to challenge or discipline their students for fear of retaliation. Raymond Lorion, a violence researcher at the University of Maryland, writes, "Many teachers suffer injuries at the hands of aggressive students. Others feel tense throughout the day."[11]

Not only do teachers fear for their own safety, but they cannot do their jobs properly because they spend much of their time dealing with angry outbursts from students, interpersonal conflicts, and inattentive students. These events severely disrupt the school day, making it difficult for students to get the education they need. A 1995 study by mental health researchers showed that exposure to violence negatively affects memory, concentration, abstract reasoning, and emotional reactivity, making learning difficult.

Even if rates of violence are lower at school than in other areas of society, everyday school violence is still a disturbing problem for too many students. In a speech before the American Federation of Teachers in July 1998, President Clinton spoke for many people when he said, "In most schools it's not the sensational acts of violence, but the smaller acts of aggression, threats, scuffles, and constant back talk that take a terrible toll on the atmosphere of learning, on the morale of teachers, on the attitudes of students."[12]

2

The Roots of
School Violence

In THE WEEKS and months after the Columbine tragedy, the nation focused on determining the causes of school violence. TV stations aired special reports, magazines published numerous articles, and newspapers explored the issue with their best reporters. People sought to understand the problem and searched for someone or something to hold responsible.

Many immediately blamed abusive homes, crime-ridden neighborhoods, hostile cultures at schools, and students' easy access to drugs and alcohol. These are commonly known as risk factors because they seem to put children at risk for becoming violent. Researchers and observers alike attempted to explain the incidents of school violence by assigning them specific risk factors. Assigning blame to one particular risk factor, however, is impossible, because not all young people who experience a particular risk factor in their lives end up committing violent acts. For example, not all students who are victims of child abuse become violent at school. For this reason, researchers must examine several risk factors when looking for the causes of school violence.

The roots of school violence are vast and complex. No one understands them fully, and no one can point to a single cause of school violence. The clearest insight researchers can offer so far is that school violence usually occurs when a combination of risk factors work together in a student's life. Some of the most common risk factors are abusive or neglectful parents, deteriorated neighborhoods, hostile school environments that breed aggression, and substance abuse.

Abuse in the home

Despite the impossibility of pinpointing a single risk factor as the cause of school violence, it is clear that certain circumstances increase one young person's likelihood to use violence at school more than another's. The most common risk factor is child abuse.

Many researchers believe that aggression begets aggression. In other words, an individual exposed to violence at an early age is more likely to become violent than someone raised in a peaceful environment. Although it is not an absolute, abuse at home is the single strongest predictor of adolescent violence.

Research shows that there are links between a student's home life and his or her tendency to be violent at school. Children who witness or experience abuse at home often

Arrested for domestic abuse, a man awaits booking by authorities. Research shows that those who were abused as children are more likely to become violent later in life than those reared in peaceful homes.

see violence as a normal solution to problems. They are more likely than children from peaceful homes to try to solve conflicts at school through aggression and violence.

In 1998, two psychiatrists at the University of Pittsburgh investigated studies dealing with the link between abusive homes and school violence. Rolf Loeber and Magda Stouthamer-Loeber found that the prevailing conclusion among the studies was that aggression at home leads to aggression at school. In fact, their research revealed that children who are both victims of abuse by a parent and witnesses of spousal abuse have a rate of assault against other children six times higher than that of children from nonassaultive families.

Not surprising, the findings for serious youth crime are similar. Charles Ewing, author of *Kids Who Kill*, writes, "The single most consistent finding regarding juvenile homicide . . . is that kids who kill . . . generally have witnessed or have been directly victimized by domestic violence."[13]

Nevertheless, researchers agree that abuse at home does not automatically lead to aggressiveness at school. Many abused children escape the violence of their home life and never become bullies or exhibit violent behavior. This is one reason why the issue is so complicated. Even though abuse at home puts a student at risk of becoming violent at school, no one can say for certain which abused students will become violent.

Neglect

Furthermore, it is not only physical abuse that sparks aggressiveness in children. Neglect is a form of psychological abuse shown to increase childhood aggression at school. Neglect occurs when parents disregard a child's needs and fail to provide the necessary supervision. Because neglectful parents are usually uninvolved in a student's life—both at school and at home—teachers generally consider this type of parent a major cause of school violence. According to a 1993 nationwide survey by Metropolitan Life, teachers regard lack of parental supervision at home as the largest contributing factor to school violence.

Certain parenting practices also put a student at risk of becoming violent at school. The Loebers' survey uncovered several parenting practices that are commonly associated with boys' aggression at school. Harsh discipline and a negative attitude toward boys under ten increased their aggression at school. Another harmful practice uncovered by the Loeber survey is coercive parenting methods that use violence or the threat of violence to force obedience from children.

Similarly, parents' inability or unwillingness to stop excessively violent conflicts between siblings at home also increased a child's aggressiveness at school. A 1982 study by three researchers found that chronic aggression between siblings may serve as a model to children for how to act toward their peers at school. The researchers conclude that "interactions with brothers and sisters usually precede interactions outside of the family and thus may serve as a bridge between the family and peer systems."[14]

What these studies don't show, however, is that raising a stable child requires more than just avoiding poor parenting practices. Researchers and educators agree that children need a role model who can provide an example of how to resolve conflicts without violence. A 1996 report in the journal *Pediatrics* found that children who lack a positive role model and are exposed to violence tend to lack the skills necessary for peaceful conflict resolution.

Overindulgent parenting

At the other end of the spectrum are parents who overindulge their children and do not provide the necessary discipline. These parents give their children everything regardless of their behavior. With such overindulgent practices, parents fail to teach their children that their actions have consequences.

Barbara Lerner, a Chicago psychologist, contends that Kip Kinkel and the Columbine gunmen, Eric Harris and Dylan Klebold, for example, were the products of overindulgent parenting. She argues that these school shooters were narcissists—people who only know self-love and never learn to love another person. Lerner believes that overindulgent parenting causes children to develop a "moral void" that makes them unable to feel empathy for other people. She writes,

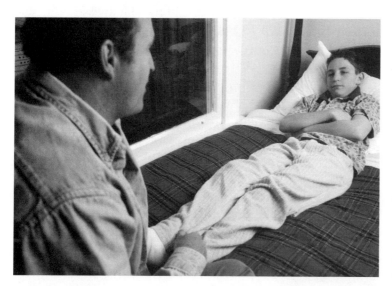

Parents who do not provide their children with the necessary discipline fail to teach their children that their actions have consequences.

Normal children learn that the parental love they could take for granted as infants and toddlers can no longer be taken for granted [as they get older]. That love is no longer unconditional; it can be withdrawn. And to avoid that frightening outcome, the child learns to see his parents as more than human pinatas, full of goodies he has only to bang away at to get. He learns to see them as moral beings with standards and values that are more important than his own immature wishes, and he begins to internalize those standards and values, making them his own, and developing a conscience.[15]

The breakdown of society

One of the ways young people develop this morality is by watching both their fathers and mothers. However, today the likelihood that a child's biological parents, nonviolent or not, will stay together is lower than ever, and researchers believe that this breakdown of the family may be linked to violent behavior. In a 1994 Gallup poll, for example, 70 percent of those surveyed believe the breakdown of the family structure contributes to school violence.

Although many children who come from single-parent families do not display aggressive behavior, the link between broken families and delinquency is strongly established. Nearly three out of four juvenile court cases involve children from single-parent homes. And studies suggest that broken families have a similar effect on school violence. In 1989, juvenile delinquency researcher D. Farrington found that separating a child from his or her parent before age ten increased aggressiveness at school during that time and predicted future school aggressiveness between the ages of twelve and fourteen.

Another risk factor for increased school violence is deteriorated neighborhoods. The surrounding community has a direct impact on a school, and violent communities may increase the violence in schools. Much of the violence found in schools originates in unhealthy, deteriorated communities. Youth violence researcher Margaret Hamburg suggests that the majority of school violence comes from violence outside schools themselves. She writes, "The problem of violence in schools is known to reflect the violence occurring in the surrounding community."[16]

Community violence infiltrates the school on the individual level—students bring it in from outside. Many children who live in and walk to school through deteriorated inner-city neighborhoods, for example, are exposed to violence and danger every day. Author James Garbarino and fellow researchers describe how children are affected by high exposure to neighborhood violence:

> Young children are enmeshed in this problem of community violence in many ways. They are witnesses to it: by age five, most [inner-city] children have had first-hand encounters with shootings. By adolescence, most have witnessed stabbings and shootings, and one-third have witnessed a homicide.[17]

Many researchers believe these neighborhoods become "natural areas for crime."[18] According to University of Maryland urban violence researcher Raymond Lorion, the violence in these crime-ridden communities shapes the attitudes of the students who live there. Lorion says that students' attitudes and behavior become "contaminated" by violent community settings. Students in turn bring the violence into their schools, where it spreads like a contagious disease. Lorion's theory is supported by the fact that the strongest predictors of school violence rates are local neighborhood crime rates.

School culture

Although many schools do reflect the communities around them, most also develop their own culture as a result of a student body that represents a variety of neighborhoods. The school itself, like a family or community, is a complete social environment with its own subtle codes of conduct. Students bring diverse outside experiences into a school, where they must interact and compete for grades and social status with others from widely different backgrounds. Because students may be used to dealing with problems at home and on the street in ways that are

Many children who walk to school through deteriorating neighborhoods are confronted by violence and danger every day.

unacceptable at school, the new school environment may cause violence to emerge.

Furthermore, a school's culture may turn violent when witnesses to aggression begin to tolerate or adopt it. When this happens, students and teachers begin to expect violence at school. Lorion studied this effect at schools and in school violence literature. He found that when the fear of violence exists at a school,

> Students tend to respond aggressively and defensively to ambiguity; teachers are likely to interpret ambiguous behaviors and situations as threatening and to anticipate violent rather than nonviolent responses. Increasingly, in such settings, the behavior of individuals becomes motivated by fear and anxiety and organized around the avoidance or control of violence, aggression, and a sense of vulnerability.[19]

Research has also found a link between violent school cultures and academic achievement. In 1994, a group of school violence researchers led by R. Felson surveyed more than twenty-two hundred students in eighty-seven different high schools and found that students who rated academic success as important also were opposed to the use of violence, whereas schools that failed to emphasize academic success fostered a greater student tolerance for violence.

Teasing undercuts identity formation

One of the most damaging behaviors to a school culture is teasing. Although there have always been bullies at school, only recently have researchers begun to look at the serious and long-term effects of bullying. What they have found is that students who are teased may develop violent habits. "All kids need to belong," New York City psychoanalyst Leon Hoffman told a *Time* reporter in 1999. "If they can't belong in a positive way at the school, they'll find a way to belong to a marginal group like a cult or a gang."[20]

Adolescence is a time when youths form their identities. Becoming a member of a group is one way an adolescent can test a new identity. Alan Leschied, a leading Canadian researcher on teen violence, says, "One of the big things with all adolescents is that, in terms of identifying with the culture, they try on different things. [The school shooters at Columbine and other schools, for example,] just tried on a very damaging identity."[21]

This may seem like a simplistic explanation, but many researchers agree that when students are teased at school, they feel as if their identity is under attack. As a result, they often feel alienated, and many victims of bullying suffer from low self-esteem. Furthermore, because teasing is often seen as a normal, childhood rite of passage, the children being teased receive little or no support from the adults around them. Rebecca Coffey, author of *Unspeakable Truths and Happy Endings*, says,

> I think kids who are teased feel extra helpless, because not only are they in a humiliating situation, but often the adults they turn to just roll their eyes and see them as perennial victims. And a whining kid becomes a kid who is difficult to love which leaves a child isolated at a time when he needs support the most. If he finds a gun, that might make him feel more powerful."[22]

Researchers have found that some students who are teased and bullied may develop violent tendencies.

Only within the last decade have researchers begun to investigate just how damaging teasing can be. One study found that 7 percent of American eighth graders stay home once a month to avoid bullies at school. Children who don't go to school not only miss out on an educational opportunity but also find themselves home alone and unhappy. All unhappy children do not turn to violence, but many violent children are unhappy. In the Loebers' survey of school violence literature, for example, they discovered that retaliation for teasing, along with retaliation for injury was the most common cause of fights at school.

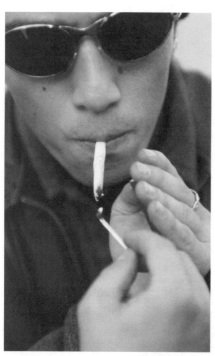

Teasing may also be a factor in some of the deadly rampages at schools. Kathy Koch, a writer for the *Congressional Quarterly*, claims that most of the five boys who went on shooting sprees in the 1997–1998 school year had been picked on and bullied. After his attack, the seventeen-year-old Pearl, Mississippi, shooter, Luke Woodham, said, "I'm not insane. I am angry. I killed because people like me are mistreated every day."[23]

Substance abuse

Another factor that puts students at risk for becoming violent is substance abuse.

Drug and alcohol use put students at risk for becoming violent.

Some students use drugs and alcohol to deal with the stress in their lives. Others may use substances for fun or because of peer pressure. Whatever the reasons, drugs and alcohol are a major risk factor for school violence. Students responding to a U.S. Department of Justice (DOJ) survey, for example, cited involvement with drugs and alcohol as the third major factor contributing to school violence.

The prevalence of drug and alcohol use by students is surprising. Many students use substances, and a large number are exposed to their sale and use. According to the National Center for Education Statistics 1999 report on school crime and safety, more than 50 percent of students in grades nine through twelve had at least one drink in the month prior to the survey. The report also stated that "The consumption of alcohol by students on school property, a crime in itself, may also lead to other crimes and misbehavior. It can lead to a school environment that is harmful to students, teachers, and staff."[24] While only 6 percent had consumed alcohol on school property, almost one-third of all students in grades nine to twelve reported they had accepted, bought, or been offered an illegal drug on school property in 1997.

Although little direct research on the link between drug use and school violence is available, numerous studies have been conducted showing that drug users are more likely to commit violent crimes. The position taken by the National Education Association (NEA) in response to these studies is unequivocal: "Users of drugs are more likely than nonusers to commit violent crime such as robberies and assaults."[25]

The unacknowledged new threat of psychotropic drugs

Most people agree that illegal drugs threaten a school's ability to provide a stable learning environment. A recent claim, however, suggests that certain prescription drugs also contribute to school violence and specifically to the deadly episodes of school shootings. Some researchers, including Kelly O'Meara, a writer for *Insight on the News*, believe there is a correlation between heavily prescribed drugs and school violence.

The connection is difficult to prove, especially with regard to the high-profile school shootings, because information about the perpetrators' medical prescriptions is protected by confidentiality laws. Nevertheless, O'Meara researched the issue and writes,

> Although the list of school-age children who have gone on violent rampages is growing at a disturbing rate—and the shootings at Columbine became a national wake-up call—few in the mental-health community have been willing to talk about the possibility that the heavily prescribed drugs and violence may be linked.[26]

These drugs, called psychotropic, are mind-altering drugs designed to treat problems such as depression, attention deficit hyperactivity disorder (ADHD), and obsessive-compulsive disorder (OCD). Six million children in the United States between the ages of six and eighteen have been prescribed psychotropic drugs. The most common are Ritalin, Prozac, and Luvox.

O'Meara says that Ritalin, specifically, has been known to produce impulsivity and violent behavior in some of the children who take it. For more than twenty years, the DOJ has listed Ritalin as a Schedule II drug, which means that it has a high potential for addiction—as high as morphine, opium, and cocaine. The International Narcotics Control Board, a United Nations agency, reported in 1995 that Ritalin's "pharmacological effects are essentially the same as those of amphetamine and methamphetamine. The abuse of [Ritalin] can lead to tolerance and severe psychological dependence. Psychotic episodes [and] violent and bizarre behavior have been reported."[27]

O'Meara also found that five of the attackers in the highly publicized school shootings in 1998–1999 were using psychotropic drugs. Kip Kinkel, for example, who murdered his parents at home and then attacked his high school in Springfield, Oregon,

Columbine gunman Eric Harris had taken a psychotropic drug prior to his shooting rampage.

where he killed two and wounded twenty-two, was taking both Ritalin and Prozac. Similarly, an autopsy of Eric Harris, one of the Columbine attackers, revealed that he had taken Luvox prior to the rampage.

Supporters of the mental health industry claim that it is not the heavy prescription of drugs causing episodes of school violence but the lack of help for young people who suffer from treatable conditions. Mike Faenza, chief executive officer of the National Mental Health Association, says, "There is little known about how the drugs affect brain function, [but] we do know that a lot of kids commit suicide because they aren't getting the help they need. It's irresponsible not to give them the help just because we don't know what causes the mental illness." [28]

No one can say for certain yet whether psychotropic drugs should join deteriorated neighborhoods, school culture, and abusive homes as a risk factor for school violence. In fact, experts commonly agree that much more research on risk factors is needed. No long-term study so far has been able to successfully separate individual, family, peer, and community influences on school violence. Since there has been a relatively small number of studies done specifically on risk factors for school violence, researchers continue to explore the topic.

3

Violence in the Media

FOR DECADES, MANY people have blamed violence in the media for real-life youth violence. More recently, parents, educators, and psychologists have focused on the media as a possible cause of school violence. They claim that young people's excessive exposure to the media in its various forms—television, movies, music, video games, and the Internet—influences how children live. And since violence exists in all of the various media, some people believe that this exposure increases the likelihood for young people to become violent at school.

The connection between media and school violence

To many parents and educators, the connection between media and school violence is obvious. They point to numerous after-school and prime-time TV programs and movies that glorify killing and violent conflict resolution. They also point to the violent music and gory video games to which many students are exposed during their free time. In fact, the National Association of Secondary School Principals maintains a straightforward stance on the issue, listing glorification of violence by the media as one of the causes of school violence.

Even though some people think the connection is obvious, it is difficult to draw a clear link between media and school violence. Since the overwhelming public interest in school violence began in the early 1990s, only a few studies have scrutinized the media specifically as a cause of the problem. What these studies found is that exposure to violent media and involvement with school violence are correlated—that is, the two are likely to occur together—but one does not necessarily cause the other. In other words, researchers have been unable to prove a direct link between media and school violence.

For example, two media violence researchers who studied high school students as early as 1972 found that the higher the violence content of their favorite TV shows, the more aggressive and likely to get into fights the students were. This does not prove, however, that watching violent TV shows made the students more aggressive at school. It only proves that aggressive students seem to watch more violent TV.

By far the majority of media violence studies focus on violent TV, movies, and music and how these three media forms affect young people in general (not just their behavior at school). Since the first studies appeared in 1955, research has commonly suggested that there is a link between media violence and youth violence and that violent images on-screen and violent lyrics in songs can influence some

Concerns about the effect of violence in the media have prompted some parents to monitor what their children watch on TV.

children to be more aggressive. In a study released in 1996, Daniel Derksen and Victor Strasburger, two researchers at the University of New Mexico Health Sciences Center, found that most of the available research supports the claim that violence in the media leads to violence in society. They write, "Over one thousand studies and reviews suggest media-portrayed violence as a cause of or contributing factor to real-life violence."[29]

Such well-known organizations as the American Medical Association, the American Psychiatric Association, and even the National Cable Television Association, among many others, have released similar findings. One TV network's own study found that one in four violent juvenile offenders had imitated crimes they saw depicted on TV.

Media researchers have also begun exploring how violent video games and violent material available on the Internet affect young people. Many parents and psychologists are concerned by the extreme amount of violence found in some of the most violent video games. They believe that video game and Internet violence are part of the reason for some of the violence occurring in schools today. Derksen and Strasburger report that video game playing is not entirely harmless: "Data extrapolated from the general media violence research suggest that violent interactive video games may cause aggressive behaviors."[30]

The extent of violence in the media

The biggest concern about media violence is that it reinforces aggressive behavior in young people. Derksen and Strasburger, for example, say that media violence affects student behavior in three ways. First, on-screen and lyrical violence models behavior for children, who may imitate it at school. Second, it reinforces aggressive behavior every time someone uses violence to solve a problem or achieve a goal. Third, it engrains the idea that violence is normal and acceptable through repetition. Derksen and Strasburger explain that "exposure to media violence influences children's violent or aggressive behavior by demonstration, reward, and practice."[31]

The amount of violence found on TV and excessive exposure to it may lead to a desensitizing effect; in other words, young viewers begin to see violence as an acceptable solution to problems. The average American child views twelve thousand murders, rapes, and assaults on TV every year. Whenever the good guys "blow away" the bad guys, the message that violence is the answer is reinforced, so much so that it becomes normal for some children.

On average, children spend less time watching movies than they do watching television, but movies tend to be more violent. For instance, the movie *Die Hard 2* portrayed 264 murders. Even though it was rated R, writer A. David suggests that ratings do not always prevent young children from viewing certain movies. David reports that the R-rated *Friday the 13th*, for example, a movie celebrated for its excessively graphic violence, was viewed by 20 percent of five- to seven-year-olds in one community.

Violent music and video games

Some researchers claim that music also contains an excess of violence. "Music is as powerful as television in its impact on people in general,"[32] writes Thomas Jipping in his research on music's effect on youth. Jipping notes that certain types of music promote extremely destructive lifestyles centered around drugs, sexual exploitation, and glamorized violence such as murder and assault.

An enormous range of violence in popular video games also concerns researchers and parents. The video game market in America is huge. Sales topped $6 billion in 1998, a large part of which came from the sale of violent video games. Violence is the main focus in forty out of forty-seven of the most popular video games. Players can choose games with hand-to-hand fighting; street fighting with sticks, knives, and clubs; and fighting using deadlier weapons such as pistols, shotguns, machine guns, and grenades.

Researchers believe that being inundated with so many violent influences in the media cannot help but affect young people's attitudes and behavior. To test this out, several researchers studied two types of communities: those to

which TV had recently been introduced and those that had decreased exposure to media violence by cutting down on TV viewing. These studies suggest a connection between TV and school violence. Derksen and Strasburger write,

> Students in communities without television scored lower in aggressiveness than those in areas with television, but quickly caught up to their peers within two years of the introduction of television. . . . Studies that eliminate or reduce exposure to television result in better classroom performance, less aggressive playground behavior, and increased family activities.[33]

Beating up on Bobo

Psychologists say that young children are most at risk for imitating behavior they witness on TV. Before about age four, children are still developing their values and their understanding of right and wrong. As part of this developmental process, they imitate behavior as they discover the relationship between action and consequence. If a child fails to receive the proper guidance during this time, he or she runs the risk of becoming violent later in life when in school. A classic study demonstrating how young children's behavior can be influenced by violent television was done in 1963. It has become known as "Beating up on Bobo."

In the study, three groups of nursery school children were shown a film in which a man walked up to an adult-sized plastic punching bag called a Bobo doll. The man ordered the Bobo doll to move out of the way. After glaring at the unresponsive doll, the man attacked Bobo, first punching it, then hitting it with a mallet, and, finally, throwing rubber balls at it. During the attack the man remarked, "Pow, right in the nose, boom, boom. . . . Sockeroo, stay down."[34] Two of the groups then each viewed a different additional segment. The first saw the man being rewarded for his actions by receiving candy. The second saw him being scolded and punished for his violent behavior. The third group saw no additional film segment.

Each child from the three groups was then individually brought into a playroom with a Bobo doll, a mallet, three balls, and other toys. There was a one-way mirror in the room so that researchers could observe the child. Almost all of the children who had seen the man punished for his violence did not repeat his actions. Many children from the other two groups, however, imitated several of his actions.

Cartoons can teach aggressiveness

The researchers reproduced the experiment with a cartoon character instead of an adult model and achieved similar results. Pediatric researchers concluded from the Bobo study that even Saturday morning cartoons, which show an average of twenty-five violent acts per hour, can teach aggressiveness to young children.

Studies such as "Beating up on Bobo" suggest how children who lack a nonviolent adult role model to provide perspective on what they watch may not learn to differentiate between media and real-life violence. Derksen and Strasburger write, "Until the age of four, many children cannot differentiate fact from fantasy, even with adult coaching. As they get older, children are better at it, but early impressions lay the foundations of the belief that the world is violent, threatening, and dangerous."[35]

When children start school, they often bring with them the belief that the world is a violent place. The violent media to which they have been exposed even before they enter kindergarten may influence their attitudes and behavior in the school environment. Derksen and Strasburger write, "Young children are particularly vulnerable; even though behaviors may not become problematic until adolescence or adulthood, they are often first manifested in school."[36]

Anecdotes are not enough

Studies on the influence that violent TV and movies have on older children are less clear. Most evidence linking media to school violence committed by older children is anecdotal—that is, it is based on stories—and is limited to high-profile school shootings.

For example, Eric Harris, one of the Columbine shooters, was fascinated with the movie *Natural Born Killers* (1994), in which a couple goes on a ferocious cross-country killing spree. According to a report in *Time* magazine, Harris studied the film closely before going on the deadly rampage at Columbine.

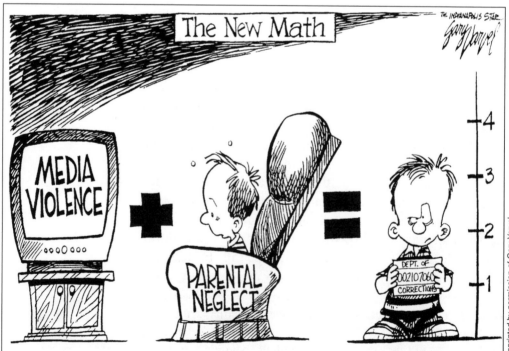

Similarly, in *The Basketball Diaries* (1995), Leonardo Di-Caprio plays a high school student who daydreams of strutting into his homeroom in a black trenchcoat and killing his teacher and fellow students with a shotgun. Fourteen-year-old Michael Carneal, who gunned down eight of his classmates in Paducah, Kentucky, claimed he may have been inspired by this scene in *The Basketball Diaries*.

As convincing as these stories may sound at first, anecdotes such as these cannot be taken as proof that media violence leads to school violence because they do not provide enough evidence to prove theories. In addition, most anecdotal evidence focuses on the highly publicized school shootings and falls short of explaining the everyday sort of violence that occurs in schools nationwide.

Michael Carneal, who shot eight of his classmates, says he may have been inspired by a scene from a recent movie in which a student daydreams of going on a killing spree.

The influence of violent music

As with TV and movie violence, much of the research linking violent music lyrics to school violence is also anecdotal and limited to headline-making incidents. However, some researchers claim that, unlike other media forms, music has the strongest influence on some students because of its ability to affect mood and behavior. Joseph Steussay, a professor of music history at the University of Texas, testified before the Senate in 1985 that "tons of research has been done on the interrelationship of music and human behavior. . . . Music affects human behavior. It affects our moods, our attitudes, our emotions, and our behavior."[37]

Numerous other researchers claim that music affects mood. They say that students who listen to music repeatedly absorb its messages. Barbara Wyatt, president of the Parents Music Resource Center, says teens "listen to music over and over. It's like listening to a foreign language over and over until it becomes part of your subconscious."[38]

The greatest concern among researchers and parents is that music's power to affect a young person's mood, when combined with violent song lyrics, may lead to real-world violence. In other words, violent lyrics may inspire some students to become violent themselves. Supporters of the music industry claim that music simply reflects the world in which it exists and that if society is violent this will naturally be recorded in the music lyrics. Some music researchers, however, claim that music does more than reflect society. Sheila Davis, professor of lyric writing at New York University, says that songs "are more than mere mirrors of society; they are a potent force in the shaping of it. . . . Popular songs provide the primary 'equipment for living' for America's youth."[39]

Internalizing music's messages

School violence researchers concerned with music's influence on students point out that young people listen to a lot of music. One study found that the average teenager listens to 10,500 hours of rock music between seventh and twelfth grades.

Jipping says that adolescents who listen to music with destructive themes tend to internalize its messages more readily. He found that "fans of rock music containing potentially negative themes (i.e., suicide, homicide, and Satanic themes) were more likely to report that they knew all of the words to their favorite songs and that the lyrics were important to their experience of the music."[40]

Music with the most violent lyrics, like gangsta rap and some heavy metal, concern the most people. These types of music tend to glorify violence. Many heavy metal song lyrics focus on satanism, drug abuse, violence, and rape. For example, Jipping says that the heavy metal band Slayer's lyrics have satanic themes and that Skid Row's lyrics are violently macho. Gangsta rap also promotes violence and romanticizes power trips of murder, sexual exploitation, and greed. Reviewers of rapper Ice Cube's 1991 platinum album found that its lyrics glorify violence and brutality.

The power to influence

The greatest concern is that music with violent lyrics has the power to influence troubled and insecure teens. Although these listeners may be in the minority, they represent a sample of young people who internalize the violent themes of music and model their behavior on its lyrics. According to Jipping, "There is a sound basis for concluding that some popular music can help lead some young people to violence."[41]

Jipping supports his claim with anecdotal evidence. For example, he says that shock-rocker Marilyn Manson tops the list of the worst offenders. Ordained as a priest in the Church of Satan, Manson's music boasts violent and destructive lyrics that deal with occultism, torture, suicide, and murder. Manson himself warns parents, "Raise your kids better or I'll raise them for you."[42]

In his study of heavy metal's influence on youth, Jipping found that at least four of the teenage killers responsible for recent school shootings idolized Manson's music. Jipping claims that Manson's music was involved in other attempts at school violence as well. For instance, five Wisconsin teens had planned a school massacre in retaliation for being teased as Manson fans, but their plot was foiled.

Singer Marilyn Manson is known for his violent and controversial lyrics.

Although these anecdotes cannot prove that violent lyrics lead to violent teenagers, they do show that music affects some young people and that violent music is sometimes linked to violent children.

Virtual violence

Unlike music and other media forms, video games offer young people the chance to participate in the action. The player becomes the main character, and in violent games, the more violence you commit, the more you're rewarded. Video game violence comes in every form imaginable, from opponents kicking, punching, and decapitating enemies in games like *Mortal Kombat* to vampires drilling partially dressed college girls through the necks with power tools in *Night Trap*. These types of video games are most popular with eight to thirteen-year-old boys, who average over four hours per week playing them.

Some psychologists claim that violent video games teach kids to kill. One of the most popular games, made by Midway Games and ID Software, is called *Quake*. It sold 1.7 million copies in its first year on the market. In it, the player becomes a lone gunman confronted by a variety of monsters. He is rewarded with points for his "kills," and as he advances, the weapons he can choose from become more deadly. Dave Grossman, a retired army officer and former psychology professor, claims that games like this "are murder simulators which over time teach a person how to look another person in the eyes and snuff their life out."[43]

Violence makes video games more exciting. One study found that almost half of all fourth through eighth graders said that their favorite electronic game was violent. However, at the same time, psychologists warn that violent video games teach young players a lack of respect for life. Grossman thinks that they have the same effect as similar military techniques used on combat soldiers: They desensitize them and "make killing a reflex action."[44] In fact, the gaming industry markets *Doom*, one of its most popular and excessively violent games, to the military for combat training.

One anecdote often cited as an example of a school gunman who learned to kill from video games is Michael Carneal. According to those who knew him, Carneal was obsessed with violent video games. Florida attorney Jack Thompson claims that, during his attack, "Carneal acted as if he were in a video game. He was simply moving his arm back and forth, picking off targets with one shot."[45] Thompson and others point out that Carneal had never fired a pistol before the day of his attack. They argue that computer games had turned him into an expert marksman since eight of the nine shots he fired struck their targets.

The electronic game industry continues to release games that are more realistic and ultraviolent. John Leo, a writer for *U.S. News & World Report*, is concerned that newer games are intent on erasing children's empathy for others. It is this lack of empathy, many researchers believe, that turns children into killers. He writes, "Some games invite players to blow away ordinary people who have done nothing wrong—pedestrians, marching bands, an elderly woman with a walker. In these games, the shooter is not a hero, just a violent sociopath."[46]

The vast majority of students do not become violent

The anecdotal evidence that media violence is linked to violent behavior at school is strong. Nevertheless, this view fails to explain the vast numbers of young people who watch TV and movies, listen to music, and play video games and never engage in violent behavior at school. Deborah Jacobs of the American Civil Liberties Union says, "Many young people view violent movies and video games, but the vast majority do not shoot up their schools as a result."[47]

Defenders of violent media forms believe that blaming their products for school violence oversimplifies the problem. Hollywood filmmakers and producers point out that movies are an easy scapegoat for violent youths who likely suffer from more severe problems than an excess of violent images in their lives. Steve Tisch, producer of *Forrest Gump* and *American History X*, asks,

> What's more troubling? A kid with a sawed-off shotgun or a kid with a cassette of *The Basketball Diaries*? It's not just movies. Lots of their wires have to short before a kid goes out and does something like this. It's a piece of a much bigger, more complex puzzle.[48]

The clearest explanation so far is that media violence is not the only cause of school violence but it may act as a contributing factor in some cases. For all the various forms, however, this view suggests that violence in the media may have its strongest influence on a small percentage of adolescents who are already troubled.

4

Gangs in Schools

GANGS ARE BECOMING increasingly prevalent on all school campuses, urban, suburban, and rural. Many law enforcement officials, educators, parents, and students are concerned about the growth of gang activity in schools. Yet the exact link between gangs and school violence remains unclear. Some people believe that gangs in schools cause increased violence, but a lack of accurate data prevents researchers from fully understanding the relationship between the two.

The violent activities of gangs, however, are well known, and many researchers and educators claim that it is common for gangs to continue these activities on school grounds. In fact, most street gangs value violence as a central part of their subculture. At school, gangs have been known to perform violent initiation rites, fight rivals, commit drive-by shootings, deal drugs, and carry weapons. Furthermore, gangs often have easy access to guns and other weapons, and they use these as they fight with competitors for control of their "turf," which sometimes includes a school campus.

The rise of gangs

Most large cities report that gangs began to pose a serious problem, on average, in 1989. The most dramatic rise of gangs in schools occurred at the beginning of the 1990s. The National Center for Education Statistics reports that gang presence at schools nearly doubled between 1989 and 1995—from 15 percent to 28 percent.

The increase of gangs in schools is a nationwide phenomenon that affects urban, suburban, and rural schools. While almost every U.S. city with a population of more than 100,000 reports having gangs, the largest recent growth of gangs in schools occurred in rural areas. According to the NCES, the number of students at rural schools who reported the presence of gangs jumped from 8 percent to 20 percent between 1989 and 1995.

Some researchers contend that this figure is misleading. They believe that rising rural gang populations are the result of non–gang members admiring and emulating gang culture. For example, researchers from the University of Nevada at Reno conducted one of the first studies looking specifically at gang involvement in rural schools, and they published their results in 1999. These researchers found that, in addition to the spread of gangs themselves, improved technology such as satellite TV and the Internet has spread gang culture and spawned "wannabes"—students merely imitating the look and behavior of gangs. They write, "Gang culture in the form of language, music, body markings, and clothing . . . has become more mainstream throughout the country, making it increasingly difficult to

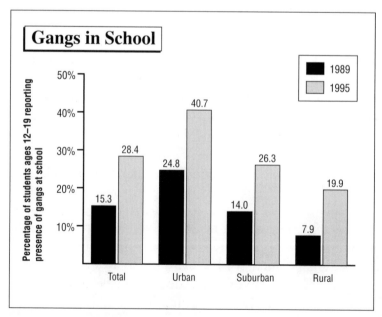

Source: National Center for Education Statistics, Bureau of Justice Statistics.

identify actual gang members from those students who may superficially identify with gang culture and fashion."[49]

The formation of gangs

These "wannabes" still pose a problem for school officials, however, because even a school with students who only imitate gang culture is at risk of gang formation. The authors of the 1993 *Handbook on Gangs in Schools* suggest that almost every school is vulnerable:

> Most schools contain at least some candidates for a future gang among their disaffected youth. All they need to get things going is a catalyst and some "street-smart" leadership. A transfer student, an acquaintance visiting from another district, a local student returning from vacation, or some disgruntled students getting together and seeking cohesive and socially disruptive outlets for their feelings could be the flash points.[50]

Some schools inherit gangs from their surrounding communities. Gangs have infested inner-city neighborhoods and schools, for example, for years, and 40 percent of students in urban areas report gangs at their schools.

Even though any school is vulnerable to gang formation, some schools are more at risk than others. For example, schools at which gangs actively recruit new members are of particular concern. The school environment is often ripe for gang recruitment because it offers a plethora of different students, some of whom may be unhappy with the school and their life circumstances and therefore easily persuaded to join a gang. Allan Hoffman and Randal Summers, two gang researchers, observe that students doing poorly or struggling with the language are prime targets for recruitment. Gangs can be ruthless in their reasons for recruiting such vulnerable students. In New Mexico, for example, assistant attorney general Joel Jacobsen found that gangs were recruiting students under thirteen as killers because the most the children could receive as punishment was two years in a juvenile facility.

The pressure to join

Many students also join gangs because of neighborhood and peer pressure. In a gang-dominated neighborhood, students have little incentive not to join, because their role models are gang members. Author James Garbarino and fellow researchers write, "Most of these children [who live in gang-infested neighborhoods] know, and in many cases depend upon, the perpetrators of community violence: gang members are also their brothers, their cousins and uncles, their fathers, or their mothers' boyfriends."[51]

It isn't only their peers who pressure children in these neighborhoods to join gangs. Fear for their own safety can influence their decision as well. For example, when one fourteen-year-old boy in Chicago received a phone call from a gang leader asking him to participate in drug dealing, the boy tried to refuse. "Well, then," the gang leader asked, "who's going to fight for you?"[52] Many children believe that without the support of the gang, they are not safe.

Students who do swear their primary allegiance to a gang may bring violence to school. One way they do this is through violent initiation rites. These rites establish a gang's reputation at school as well as induct new student members into the gang. The *Handbook on Gangs in Schools* explains that new recruits are

> required to show their prowess by fighting several members or running a gauntlet (members beat up on the recruit to see if he [can] take it). This practice is known as "courting" or being "jumped" into the gang. Members are "courted" or "jumped" in and out of the gang regularly on school campuses, especially during lunch time.[53]

Gang violence at school

The toughness and fighting skills that are valued so highly by gangs often conflict with the peaceful learning environment needed in schools. When these two cultures clash, the results are often violent. A 1990 study by gang researcher I. Spergel found that, although gang members made up only a small percentage of the student population he studied, gangs were responsible for a disproportionately high percentage of serious school crime: 12 percent of the weapons violations, 26 percent of the robberies, and 20 percent of the aggravated assaults.

Because of this high participation in crime and violence, gangs sometimes disrupt education to the point of paralyzing an entire school with fear. In 1990, a gang riot erupted at Cleveland High School in Reseda, California, that involved more than two hundred students. After the riot, students avoided certain hallways for fear of being jumped. "Explosive situations were just below the surface," says Barbara Yannuck, a drama teacher at Cleveland High for twenty-two years. "It wouldn't take much— a casual remark, playing the wrong kind of music—to set them off."[54]

Gangs can also pose a serious threat to student safety. In another instance of gang violence on school property, rival gangs exchanged gunfire after a football game between Dorsey High and Crenshaw High in Los Angeles. Two uninvolved student bystanders were caught in the crossfire and shot.

A month later, parents of players from a rival football team refused to let their children play in a game against Dorsey High. Even though the game was to match the two best teams in L.A. against each other, the parents refused out of fear of gang violence. School officials at Dorsey High warned that forgoing the football game would be a victory for gangs but, in the end, the high school game was canceled.

While gangs make up only a small percentage of the student population, gang members are responsible for a disproportionately high percentage of serious crimes at schools.

The role of schools

Some educators say that the schools themselves are partly to blame for gang violence on campus. They further claim that schools are responsible when students join gangs. If a school repeatedly labels students as failures and does not provide the support its struggling students need to succeed, they may turn to gangs. For example, at Webb Middle School in Austin, Texas, gangs were already a problem in and around the school when it hired a new principal, Tina Juarez. She quickly found that students who felt like academic failures at school could easily join gangs. In fact, after receiving an F grade just one time, some students at Webb gave up trying in their classes and eventually joined gangs. They felt like failures in school, but in the gang they had value. One day, a boy in her office explained to Juarez, "Miss, in school we are 'nothings.' In a gang, we are somebodies."[55] Though the situation at Webb Middle School shows an extreme example of students driven to gangs by academic failure, it symbolizes the problem other schools face.

Researchers also contend that schools can promote social rejection of students by failing to identify their at-risk students and giving them help. With the breakdown of the family, students look to peers, teachers, and organizations at school such as clubs and sports teams to give them a sense of belonging and self-identity. When school officials ignore warning signs, some researchers believe, they may lose their students to a gang that values their membership. Luis Rodriguez, for example, became involved with drugs and violence as a student and gang member in Los Angeles. In an interview for the National Education Association, he says,

> Gangs aren't alien powers. They begin as unstructured groupings, but they attract children who want the same things as any young person: respect. A sense of belonging. Protection. The same things that those who join the YMCA, Little League, or the Boy Scouts want.[56]

Researchers have found that gangs often take on a pseudo-family role for student members. This is especially true for students who lack a father figure, as do many gang members. They may find a sense of family that they don't get at home. Gangs fulfill important needs for their members that have gone unmet elsewhere and, for those students who join, the gang becomes their family. One gang member told a reporter that his gang "is a second family in a sense. I was always with [the gang], spending more time with them than at home."[57]

There is also evidence that schools provide settings that lend themselves to violent gang activity. Rolf Loeber and Magda Stouthamer-Loeber, child psychiatry experts at the

University of Pittsburgh, found that when several young children "gang up on" a single child, they may be exhibiting early ganglike behavior. This means that children left unsupervised, on the playground, for example, may provide the opportunity for informal groups of students to victimize helpless students. This early aggressive behavior is called "ganging" or "mobbing" and is probably unique to schools because other environments (home, for example) tend not to provide the opportunity. As a result, the Loebers conclude, schools may unknowingly give young students the opportunity to explore the feelings of power and violence that are central to the gang experience.

Teens sometimes turn to gangs to fulfill their need for a sense of family that they may lack at home.

Gangs sell drugs at school

The school setting also provides a prime market for selling drugs, and most gangs rely on the income from selling drugs to support themselves. In fact, 60 percent of gang members admit to selling drugs at school. According to Thomas Capozzoli and Steve McVey, authors of a book on managing gangs in schools, many gang members stay in

Some educators have observed that teens who feel like academic failures will sometimes join a gang to gain a sense of worth.

school simply so that they can continue to sell drugs to students. Capozzoli and McVey write, "Gangs are many times involved in the trafficking of drugs and weapons and the fact that they are present in a school can increase the tensions for everyone in the school."[58]

Drug selling at school brings with it violence and fear. To sell drugs at school, gangs must establish a "turf," or area they claim as their own, and maintain dominance over that "turf." One way gangs establish territory, according to the authors of the *Handbook on Gangs in Schools*, is by regularly gathering in a particular place on the school campus as a show of force. This activity is known as "milling," and it increases the fear of gang violence at a school. The authors write,

> At school, [gang members] stake out certain unofficial designated areas; unofficial because school officials neither prohibit nor sanction the member-designated gathering places. Milling occurs before and after school, but mostly during events and lunch time when a large audience will see them. Lunch benches, bleachers, and playing fields are popular hangouts, and once these areas are "claimed," other students will not intrude.[59]

Gangs also establish territory for selling drugs by fighting with rival gangs and other drug sellers at school. Once dominance of the drug market at a particular school is established, a gang must continually guard against invasion into its selling territory. Students can be caught in the middle of territorial drug wars at school; these wars can include fistfights, knives, or even guns.

Locura violence

Students can also become victims of random, senseless acts of violence committed by gang members. This type of violence is known as *locura,* or "extremely crazy," violence. *Locura* violence is a sign of a gang's capacity for unrestrained and unprovoked violence and is used to establish dominance over a particular territory by demonstrating that the gang is extremely dangerous and not to be crossed. Innocent students can become victims of *locura* violence, which increases the level of fear at a school.

Although there are no official statistics on how commonly *locura* violence occurs in schools, gang members themselves admit to assaulting students. It is likely that some of the assaults are the result of gangs establishing and defending their territory to sell drugs, but many others are just random attacks. In a 1996 study in the research journal *Education and Urban Safety*, two researchers

Three Los Angeles gang members show off their arsenal of dangerous weapons.

surveyed youth gang members in Cleveland, Denver, and south Florida. They report that 70 percent of respondents claimed their gangs assaulted students. This includes all types of attacks, *locura* and otherwise.

Gangs increase weapon carrying at school

Gangs also increase weapon carrying in schools. The same study in *Education and Urban Safety* found that more than 80 percent of the gang members surveyed claimed to have brought knives and guns to school. Two girls in a Brooklyn street gang called the MGBs, for example, carried X-acto knives to school as weapons. They wrapped them in cardboard to elude the metal detector.

The presence of gangs may cause other students to carry weapons out of fear for their own safety. Capozzoli and McVey write, "Even though the gang may not be the impetus of the violence, students arm themselves for protection from gangs and this could indirectly cause some form of violence."[60]

In addition, gangs have begun using more sophisticated weapons than ever before. Huge profits from selling drugs, especially crack cocaine, have made more expensive, deadlier weapons available to gang members. The *Handbook on Gangs in Schools* states, "Today's gangs are highly mobile, well armed, high tech, and generously funded."[61] In the past, gangs fought with baseball bats and knives, but now they have access to semiautomatic and assault rifles such as AK-47s and Uzis. These are the weapons of choice for drive-by shootings, and some inner-city schools experience drive-bys so often that they have added drive-by shooting drills to their traditional fire drills.

Although there are no official statistics as evidence, many people believe that gangs also sell guns to students. Similar to their trade in drugs, gangs may sell illegal weapons, often stolen guns. These guns are available sometimes for as little as $50. In a survey conducted by Tulane University researchers Joseph Sheley and Dwayne Smith, two-thirds of suburban high school students reported that they would have only "a little trouble" obtaining a gun.[62]

Gang violence at schools is mostly hype

Despite the widespread concern over gangs in schools, some researchers believe that gangs do not significantly contribute to the problem of school violence. Douglas Clay and Frank Aquila, researchers at Cleveland State University, for instance, claim that school officials, parents, and police officers are overreacting to the gang problem.

Clay and Aquila argue that the widespread publicity on gangs has led to an unfounded fear of their presence in schools. Although the two researchers do not offer statistics to support their claims, they believe that most school officials mistakenly assume they have a gang problem when only superficial evidence of gangs exists. They write,

> School board members, administrators, and teachers must remember that the wearing of "gang" clothing or the appearance of "gang" graffiti does not always translate into gang activity and crime. In reality, the so-called national spread of gang problems may be nothing more than another teenage fad—the 1990s version of the hula hoop or the pet rock.[63]

Clay and Aquila further argue that the hype around gangs in schools has taken the focus away from the important issues of school safety. According to them, the idea that organized gangs recruit from schools is a myth and efforts aimed at preventing gang violence in schools really only help to "spread the gang lit[erature]." They write, "We are allowing the titillating and sordid details of gang lore to take our eyes off the ball of school safety and security. We need to spend our time combating real problems and not fighting bogeymen."[64]

While researchers such as Clay and Aquila offer a reminder that superficial signs of gangs at a school do not always translate into the presence of hardcore street gangs in the hallways, it is difficult to ignore the overwhelming number of students nationwide who report gangs at their schools. Furthermore, the fear of gangs at school is well documented, as is the shocking number of guns and other weapons being brought to school every day, by both gang members and students not in gangs.

5

Guns in Schools

A HIGH-PROFILE SCHOOL shooting inevitably reignites a nationwide discussion about gun control. Each tragedy brings heightened public concern and immediate pressure for politicians to enact policies to reduce the violence in schools. For instance, on April 30, 2000, when a six-year-old boy shot and killed his first-grade classmate in Michigan, public outrage erupted. People were shocked that a boy so young would have access to a loaded pistol and be able to bring it to school.

Many people believe that guns are too accessible and that new laws should be created to restrict access to handguns. According to Michael Hinds, a writer for the journal *American Demographics*, the overwhelming majority of Americans support new restrictions on handguns. In fact, new gun control legislation has appeared in several states, but primarily only in response to high-profile school shootings and the anniversaries of such tragedies.

While it is obvious that guns play a role in school violence, it is still not known whether gun control is really a solution to the problem. There is no conclusive evidence that tighter gun control would reduce the violence occurring in America's schools.

An alarming number of guns

Today, researchers estimate that there are close to 200 million guns owned by private citizens in the United States. Sixty-five million of these are handguns—pistols or revolvers. Since it is illegal for anyone under eighteen to own a handgun in the United States, any pistol that makes its way into a school must have started out in the hands of an adult. Only adults can legally purchase handguns. Nevertheless, juveniles possess them at an unprecedented rate; more youths are using guns in crimes than ever before. Between 1985 and 1994, the number of adolescents who killed with a gun quadrupled, while the number murdering with other types of weapons remained the same.

Many of these students and their guns make their way into schools every day. Some guns travel in backpacks along with homework and pencils. Others remain in lockers, waiting to be used. In the 1996–1997 school year, nearly 1 million kids brought a gun to school, and every day kids across the country bring an estimated total of 270,000 guns to school.

Students bring guns to school for different reasons. Gang members may be required to carry a gun as a condition of membership. Other students carry guns because it gives them a sense of power and control. Still others carry guns for protection. "When they believe the world is a dangerous place, many children take the offensive,"[65] says Carolyn Newberger of Boston Children's Hospital.

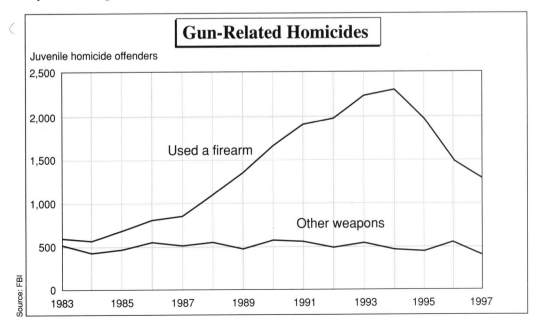

Gun-Related Homicides

Handgun Control Inc. (HCI), the leading gun control advocacy group, argues that weak gun laws are fueling the epidemic of guns in schools. Dennis Henigan, director of legal affairs for HCI, says, "In most states it's perfectly legal for a licensed dealer to sell 15 to 20 handguns to a single purchaser. Then [they] turn around and sell those guns in the black market."[66] Young people can buy stolen and black market guns on the street for as little as $50.

Deadly consequences

Gun control advocates claim that the ready availability of guns in society guarantees that some will be misused—with deadly consequences. With such easy access to a deadly weapon, a troubled or scared student may see a gun as a simple solution to a problem. A student under stress may not think through the consequences of his or her actions and choose a permanent, deadly solution to a temporary problem. Bill Smith, a history teacher at Thurston High School, where Kip Kinkel opened fire in the cafeteria, killing two and wounding twenty-two, writes,

> It should be obvious that legislation decreasing kids' exposure to guns will positively affect the safety of our schools. For much too long, we have allowed ourselves to believe there is no correlation between a society with extremely accessible firearms and deadly violence. Children without access to their parents' firearms or illegal guns will be less likely to commit violent acts with guns at school.[67]

Gun control groups point out that the disputes between young people are no different now than in the past. What *has* changed, they say, is the availability of guns. Gun control advocates do not deny that American culture can produce violent fantasies in the minds of youths, but they argue that, without the hardware, troubled youths cannot make their fantasy a reality.

Groups such as HCI also point out that easy access to guns allows an angry student to use deadly violence. Whereas in the past an angry student might have used less deadly fists or weapons such as clubs and knives, today kids are more likely to rely on firearms. Curt Lavarello, executive director of the National Association of School Resource Officers and a police officer who worked for twelve years in schools, claims that tightened gun control laws would decrease deadly school violence. He says, "A lot of the issues that kids get into fights over are the same as they were 25 years ago. What's changed drastically is the availability and accessibility of weapons and firearms, and the desire to turn to weapons to end a dispute."[68]

In the case of killings by young children, gun control advocates argue that easy access to firearms is the obvious culprit. They claim that a young child such as the six-year-old boy in Michigan cannot fully comprehend the consequences of his actions. This is why it is especially important to keep guns away from young children. Besides not understanding a gun's deadly power, young children often mistake it for a toy. Author Charles Ewing writes,

Easy availability of guns in the home is unquestionably a major factor in homicides committed by preteens. . . . What all these killings have in common is that they would not have occurred had the young perpetrators not had ready access to guns and ammunition.[69]

Tighter controls

Students' ready access to firearms and the alarming number of guns in schools have led to calls for tighter gun controls. Many people believe that passing laws that make it harder to buy guns and that require owners to store them safely will reduce gun violence in schools. Gun control advocates are becoming more vocal and influential. On May 14, 2000, for example, about 750,000 people gathered in Washington, D.C., for the Million Mom March to protest the lack of effective gun controls. The march attracted national attention, and its organizers credit the gathering for the subsequent passage of gun legislation in the Senate and in New Hampshire and New Jersey.

As a result of public pressure, some states have begun tightening their gun laws. Since the Columbine tragedy, for example, the nation has focused on Colorado's efforts to improve gun safety. In 1999, Colorado governor Bill Owens recommended five new gun restrictions. He suggested opening juvenile records for background checks on gun purchases; banning "straw purchases," or buying a gun for someone else who legally cannot; requiring background checks for purchases at gun shows; raising the legal age for buying a handgun from eighteen to twenty-one, and requiring safe storage of guns in homes.

In addition, in April 2000 Maryland became the first state to require built-in locks on handguns. The Maryland measure is one of the toughest gun control laws in the nation, a result of public pressure to stop gun violence in schools. "It's clear," says Caspar Taylor, a Democratic legislator from Maryland, "that the entire country now sees gun violence as a top priority."[70]

It is too soon to know if any of these gun control measures will have an effect on school violence. Some research does suggest, however, that there is a correlation

Gun control advocates demonstrate at a rally held near the National Rifle Association's headquarters in Washington, D.C.

between tightened gun controls and decreased youth violence in general. In other words, a few studies show that juvenile gun crime has decreased at the same time that some states have tightened their gun restrictions. For example, since neighboring Maryland and Virginia passed tightened gun controls, Washington, D.C., experienced a 63 percent decline in juvenile homicide arrests.

Nationally, a similar correlation has been reported. The most recent statistics suggest that the new gun restrictions and public concern about gun violence, as well as the increased economic conditions for teenagers, are having positive effects. Juvenile homicide decreased 44 percent in the United States from 1996 to 1999.

Ineffective legislation?

Pro-gun groups disagree with these statistics, saying that past gun laws do not seem to have been effective and that it is unlikely that further gun control will reduce school violence. Groups such as the Gun Owners of America (GOA) point out that, if gun restrictions actually decreased violence, juvenile crime should have plummeted after the passage of the Gun Control Act in 1968, which made it illegal for anyone under eighteen to own a handgun. "If the gun control theory had any merit," says John Velleco, a spokesman for GOA, "we should have had more shootings by juveniles before 1968 and then it should have declined. But that didn't happen."[71]

The National Rifle Association (NRA) also says that new gun laws are not what is needed since present laws already make it illegal to bring a gun to school. The Gun-Free Schools Act passed by Congress in 1994 prohibits anyone from bringing a firearm to school. Tanya Metaksa, former chief lobbyist for the NRA, says, "No amount of laws are going to stop a juvenile or adult from illegally procuring a gun or knife or anything else."[72]

The NRA and pro-gun groups further claim that laws will not prevent students who have their mind set on committing a criminal act from carrying out their plans. Metaksa says that a student who really wants to kill or injure someone will always be able to find a gun and a law will not stop him or her. She points out that, prior to their attack in Jonesboro, Arkansas, that killed four classmates and a teacher, school shooters Andrew Golden and Mitchell Johnson tried to blow-torch their way into a gun safe. When that didn't work, the boys broke into Golden's grandfather's house and stole seven guns. "Gun control works with people who obey laws," writes Don Feder, a syndicated columnist for the *Boston Herald* who believes that gun control is not the answer to the problem of school violence. "People with murderous impulses, adults or kids, will always find a way to get guns."[73]

Does gun control avoid the real problems?

Gun advocates like Feder and Metaksa say that enacting stricter gun laws only avoids the real problems at the heart of school violence. They say that school violence is a problem not rooted in easy access to guns but in other defects of American society. Alan Gottlieb, chairman of the Citizens Committee for the Right to Keep and Bear Arms, sees the new gun restrictions as attempts at a quick fix to the large and complex problem of school shootings. "The knee-jerk reaction to impose more gun controls in the wake of these incidents fails to address the underlying problem," he says. "Gun control is a Band-Aid approach to a potentially serious hemorrhage."[74]

Instead of ready access to firearms, gun advocates suggest that several other problems lie at the roots of school violence. One of these is what researchers see as a new code of conduct among today's teenagers. Researchers like

Pro-gun groups argue that past gun laws have been ineffective at reducing school violence.

Thomas Toch and Marc Silver, writers for *U.S. News & World Report*, say that students have become desensitized to pain and killing and are less hesitant to use deadly force to solve their problems. They argue that the problem of gun violence in schools is not due to easy access to firearms but, instead, to a readiness to pull the trigger. "Behind the rash of violence," Toch and Silver write, "is a startling shift in adolescent attitudes. Suddenly—chillingly—respect for life has ebbed sharply among teenagers—and not just in embattled inner cities."[75]

Many politicians believe that negligent adults are the problem. Statistics support their claim since four out of five of the guns brought to school are from students' homes. Senator Richard Durbin of Illinois believes that parents should be held accountable if a child gains access to unsecured guns in the home. Many legislators agree with him, and sixteen states have child access prevention (CAP) laws on their books. CAP laws make gun owners liable if they fail to store their firearms properly and a juvenile uses them to commit a crime. Senator Durbin says, "It's time for the adults who own the guns to act responsibly, to store them safely and to take responsibility for the guns in their possession."[76]

A weak justice system fails to deter school violence

Another source of gun violence in schools, claims the NRA and other pro-gun groups, is a weak juvenile justice system. The NRA believes that juveniles who commit adult crimes such as murder and illegal possession of a handgun should be tried as adults. A federal study of juvenile courts in the early 1990s found that less than one-third of juveniles accused of a violent crime stayed in custody; the rest were either released or put on probation.

The NRA uses the case of Kip Kinkel to argue that the current juvenile justice system is ineffective in preventing school violence. The day before his rampage, Kinkel was arrested at Thurston High School for buying a stolen pistol. Instead of being kept in custody, however, he was released and carried out his attack at the school the next morning. The NRA points out that had Kinkel been kept in custody and his case examined more closely, officials would have recognized his potential for violence. At the very least, the NRA says, he would not have been able to act so impulsively.

The NRA also supports the philosophy of "adult crime, adult time," which means that students who commit serious violent crimes at school and elsewhere should be prosecuted as adults since these are typically adult crimes. The NRA and gun advocates claim that getting tough on "kid killers" who attack schools will deter other students from committing serious acts of school violence.

A lack of enforcement of existing gun laws

Strict enforcement of existing laws could also go a long way toward lowering school gun violence. Plenty of laws already exist to keep guns out of schools, but police and the government fail to enforce them. Without adequate enforcement, the laws fail to act as deterrents to potential young school shooters. Wayne LaPierre, executive director of the NRA, says the real problem with guns in schools

Executive director of the NRA, Wayne LaPierre (right), and NRA president Charleton Heston.

> is the complete collapse of enforcement of the existing firearm laws on the books by the Department of Justice. The proof is in the statistics. Six thousand kids illegally brought guns to school the last two years. We've only had 13 [federal] prosecutions. And only 11 prosecutions for illegally transferring guns to juveniles.[77]

Despite these claims by pro-gun groups, new gun control laws have been passed by several states in response to school shootings, and new legislation is appearing at the federal level. The public outrage at guns in schools has brought about new gun restrictions. This is one of several ways society and schools are attempting to deal with the problem of school violence.

6

Making Schools Safe

S<small>INCE</small> THE EARLY 1990s, school safety has become a top priority across the nation. Schools, communities, lawmakers, and even students are working to stop the violence in schools. Separately and together they are using many different approaches to curb school violence.

Schools reacted by increasing security and implementing a variety of violence prevention programs. Parents and communities in many school districts also came together to create violence prevention programs tailored to the particular needs of their local schools. Lawmakers passed bills in the 1990s specifically designed to reduce school violence. A large majority of students also expressed a willingness to take an active stand against violence, and students at some schools even formed antiviolence groups.

Studies indicate that these violence prevention efforts may be working in some cases because school violence overall is not increasing. In fact, schools became somewhat safer during the 1990s. The September 1999 School Crime and Safety Report by the National Center for Education Statistics indicates that, between 1993 and 1997, nonfatal student victimization rates at schools across the country declined.

Not all types of school violence declined, however. Some have stayed constant, meaning that the violence prevention efforts of schools, lawmakers, and communities may not be reducing the problem as much as planned. For example, the number of students who were threatened with or injured by a weapon at school and the number who were

in a fight on school grounds both remained constant between 1993 and 1997.

Violence prevention starts in the schools

Schools were the first to react to school violence and
have introduced the most programs to combat the problem.
The most common strategy schools have used is to imple-
ment programs aimed at stopping violence before it ever
happens. These are called violence prevention programs. A
1998 NCES study found that more than three out of four
public schools have such a program in place.

The most popular violence prevention program is conflict resolution because it seems to have numerous benefits.
Dr. Deborah Prothrow-Stith, a nationally renowned scholar
on violence prevention, and Sher Quaday, director of violence prevention programs at the Harvard School of Public
Health, report that, in general, the short-term evaluations of
conflict resolution programs appear promising. They write
that, as a result of conflict resolution curricula, "positive effects have been seen . . . on student knowledge, attitudes,
and behavior; teacher attitudes and competence in violence-
prevention skills; school climate; school statistics in vio-
lence/misbehavior . . . and general support of programs."[78]

*Fifth graders learn
problem-solving skills
during a conflict
resolution class.*

Conflict resolution programs teach students to find nonviolent solutions to problems. Students learn peaceful responses to threats and teasing. They also role-play and videotape pretend fights to help them understand that violence arises from peer pressure and a lack of emotional control. "When somebody tries to talk trash to me, about my mother or whatever, I just don't say anything," says one sixteen-year-old student in a conflict resolution program who lives in a rough neighborhood in Boston. "I'm a brick wall. And they get bored and go away because I won't let them push me into doing something I don't want to do, which is to talk trash back at them and give them something to get madder about. Why would I do that? It's stupid."[79]

One successful conflict resolution program called Second Step teaches students empathy, impulse control, and anger management. Holli McKelvey, who trains school staff on how to use Second Step, says the program shows students "that anger develops in stages, from feeling mildly irritated, to being really mad, to reaching a boiling point. We focus on how the body gives us signs and cues that anger is rising, by things like sweaty palms or clenched fists."[80] At Deerfield Elementary in Maryland, the Second Step program helped reduce the suspension rate by 65 percent.

Increased security as a further precaution

In addition to programs aimed at giving students the tools for dealing with aggressive behavior, many schools have increased security as a further precaution. Many schools hired more security officers. Some schools hired peace officers who patrol the hallways as security guards but also teach students about violence prevention. For security alone, New York City schools spend more than $43 million a year.

A security strategy used by many large urban schools is to screen students using metal detectors. Some schools use handheld wands to do random checks on students, while at other schools students must pass through metal detectors each day. Almost one in six schools with one thousand students or more uses metal detectors.

Despite the popularity of metal detectors at large schools, many educators and researchers question their effectiveness. A 1993 article in the *Economist* claims that

> The trouble with metal detectors . . . is that they are expensive ($10,000 for the walk-through variety, and $17,000 if it is equipped with an X-ray), unpopular (parents complain that they make schools look like prisons), intrusive (in Thomas Jefferson High [in Brooklyn, New York,] it takes from 7:30 a.m. to 10:00 a.m. to check all 3,000 students) and frequently ineffective (students hide weapons outside school, in rubbish bins and on waste ground, and then smuggle them in through windows).[81]

Many large urban schools now use metal detectors as a precaution against school violence.

Zero tolerance

School officials nationwide have also made an effort to clearly state their views on bringing weapons to school, which has resulted in immediate suspension for a student caught carrying a weapon at school, drinking alcohol, using or selling drugs, or fighting on school grounds. Committing an offense just once can result in a suspension of six months or even expulsion.

Critics complain that these policies, called zero-tolerance policies, are an overreaction to the problem and too extreme. They warn that overzealous school officials can abuse zero tolerance. For example, a fourteen-year-old boy with a clean discipline record received an assignment in his English class at a junior high in Virginia. He was to write an essay by finishing the following sentence: "If I could do anything to this school, I would . . ." The boy wrote "Blow it up"[82] to start his essay and went on to explain how he would rebuild the school with high-quality laboratories and the best science teachers. When his teacher and school authorities read the essay, the boy was arrested, suspended for ten days, and threatened with jail.

Many schools, like the junior high in Virginia, adopted a no-nonsense, zero-tolerance policy on threats. Out of a

desire to quickly crack down on potential perpetrators of school violence, these schools strictly enforced the new policies, in many cases suspending and expelling students who had committed either no intentional offense or only a minor one like bringing a squirt gun to school. "The major challenge for schools," says Ronald Stephens, executive director of the National School Safety Center (NSSC), "is how to react without overreacting."[83]

In addition, opponents countered that zero-tolerance policies can put communities at risk. If a student is expelled for bringing a gun to school, then the community suddenly has an armed juvenile on its streets. However, some schools working with their communities have developed programs to combat this problem and prevent students from being home alone or free in the neighborhood during their suspension or expulsion. In these cases, the students are sent to an alternative school to study self-control and violence prevention.

Other school-based strategies

Since each school is unique and has its own problems with violence, different strategies are being tried in different school districts around the country. One strategy introduced in some urban areas is school uniforms. Many students are against wearing uniforms to school because they feel that uniforms infringe on their right to individual freedom of expression. Nevertheless, uniforms have several benefits: They prevent the wearing of gang colors, reduce students' ability to carry concealed weapons, and minimize peer pressure. At the same time, they foster school pride and make it easier for school personnel to identify intruders. The year after Long Beach, California, instituted school uniforms, fights and weapon carrying dropped 50 percent. Other schools report similar results.

Another inexpensive and successful program is a telephone hotline for anonymous tips about violence. The Safe Schools Hotline is used by more than eight hundred school

Schools that have implemented school uniforms report a sharp decline in fighting and weapon carrying.

systems in nine states. A caller talks to a central computer in Columbus, Ohio, and the information is then faxed to local school authorities. The caller receives a four-digit case number and is asked to call back within three days for an update or to provide further information. "It's a fantastic concept," says Paul Kitchen, assistant superintendent of Sikerton Public Schools in Missouri, which uses the hotline. "I've never seen a better program for the money. You can't get enough police officers and metal detectors to solve this problem."[84]

Psychological profiling is another strategy some schools use to identify alienated and troubled students before they commit a violent act, although it has been less successful. In reexamining several cases of school shootings, organizations like the NSSC in Westlake Village, California, found that many of the school gunmen displayed similar early warning signs. As a result the NSSC and other agencies such as the FBI developed a checklist of warning signs that teachers can use to identify potentially troubled and violent students. The U.S. Department of Education (DOE) distributes these checklists to teachers across the nation. The NSSC checklist includes characteristics such as "Reflects anger, frustration and the dark side of life in school essays or writing projects; Tends to blame others for difficulties and problems he causes himself; Has serious disciplinary problems at school and in the community."[85]

Critics of psychological profiling claim that it is a breach of student privacy and an invasion of their rights. They point to school districts such as the one in Granite City, Illinois, which keeps a computerized behavior file on every student from kindergarten through twelfth grade, recording such incidents as bullying and if a student's sibling is caught with a weapon at school. A student who has access to guns and writes about the "dark side of life" can be expelled or required to undergo counseling. Kevin Dwyer, president of the National Association of School Psychologists, says,

> The problem with this whole [profiling] thing is that if you're dealing with a serial killer and have 25 suspects and you can see a pattern, that might be something useful. But when

you're talking about 53 million children and putting this in the hands of people who don't understand the material . . . you're going to do irreparable harm.[86]

Violence prevention in the classroom

Teachers are also playing an important role in preventing school violence. Because they can get to know students well, teachers sometimes can identify troubled and potentially dangerous students well before any irreparable violence occurs. Mary Futrell, a respected violence researcher, writes,

> Teachers see the negative and positive sides of student behavior and attitudes long before school boards or central administrators or the community become alarmed and decide to act. Teachers know the symptoms long before the metal detectors, security guards, or random searches become part of the school environment. Teachers see signs of disruptive, even violent, behavior as early as preschool and elementary school.[87]

Teachers have become increasingly aware of the warning signs of potentially violent students and are more vigilant

Teachers can play an important role in preventing school violence by recognizing the warning signs of violent behavior in students and intervening when necessary.

than ever in observing student behavior. They are often the first to catch infractions o ny mention of violence in their classrooms, including notes passed between students and drawings with violent acts.

Despite these positive intentions, such vigilance on the part of teachers does run the risk of overreaction. While the DOE recommends that school authorities intervene immediately if a student has a weapon or presents a detailed plan for violence, it also warns that teachers must not misinterpret student behavior and punish developmentally typical behavior.

One English teacher who works at an alternative school with her community's most troubled youths tries to avoid overreaction by establishing a contract with her students to make their classroom a neutral, violence-free zone. Eva Kendrick invites her students to participate in decision making about how to make their classroom an effective learning environment. She has them discuss and write about what roles they think the teacher and students should have in creating a nonviolent classroom. By using a more democratic teaching style, Kendrick has been successful in reducing vandalism and disruptions in her classroom.

Federal legislation

Almost all violence prevention programs require money, and as the public and lawmakers become more concerned about school violence, new initiatives and funding are being sponsored at the federal level to meet schools' needs. In 1994, Congress adopted the Goals 2000: Educate America Act, which states that "no child or youth should be fearful on the way to school, be afraid while there, or have to cope with pressures to make unhealthy choices."[88] This act provided $630 million in federal grants to schools and communities to improve school safety. It also allotted $50 million to schools with the worst crime problems.

In addition to providing money for improved school safety, federal legislators have passed laws designed to reduce school violence, primarily by controlling guns. High-profile school shootings immediately led to demands at the federal level to broaden gun restrictions. As a result, in 1990 Congress created the Gun-Free School Zones Act and made it a felony for anyone to bring a gun within one thousand feet of any American school. The Supreme Court overturned this act in 1994, ruling that the act was unconstitutional and that Congress had exceeded its authority. In the same year, however, Congress passed the Gun-Free Schools Act, which requires a mandatory one-year expulsion for any student caught with a gun at school. As a result of this second act, sixty-one hundred students were expelled for bringing a gun to school during the 1996–1997 school year.

State legislation

States are also legislating to stop school violence. Almost every state in the United States changed its laws in the 1990s to improve the problem of youth violence. Many states are adopting so-called get-tough laws that lower the age at which violent young people can be tried as adults.

Students and adults gather in Washington, D.C., to convince federal legislators to increase gun restrictions.

Although these laws are popular with the public, experts warn that such strategies "are designed to respond to violence after it has occurred rather than to prevent its occurrence in the first place." Futrell says, "The get-tough strategies being implemented in many communities are deemed necessary but are woefully insufficient."[89]

States have also increased gun restrictions in an attempt to reduce school and youth violence. In April 2000, for example, Maryland passed the toughest gun-lock law in history. It became the first state to require safety devices to be sold with all handguns. The law also requires that, by 2003, built-in locks must be implemented on all new handguns sold in the state.

Concerned parents take action

Many of the demands for legislation to reduce school violence come from parents concerned for their children's safety at school. Besides helping to reduce school violence this way, some concerned parents have also taken an active role at their children's schools by volunteering to be members of parent safety teams. These teams patrol the school's hallways and monitor student behavior.

Experts explain that the mere presence of parent volunteers at school leads to improved student behavior. In 1994, for example, when a teenager was shot near one of the most violent high schools in Baton Rouge, Louisiana, the parents and school instituted a "Dads Patrol." Several fathers purchased matching T-shirts and appeared at the school every day. School officials note that the "Dads Patrol" did not have to deal with many violent incidents; their presence was enough to improve student behavior.

At many schools, parents can also receive training in violence prevention. The Resolving Conflict Creatively Program (RCCP), begun in Brooklyn, New York, offers workshops to parents nationwide that focus on peaceful conflict resolution. Nearly two thousand parent leaders across the country have been trained to lead RCCP workshops. An evaluation of New York City's RCCP by Metis Associates, Inc., found decreased violence among stu-

dents. In 1990, 71 percent of the teachers surveyed reported that RCCP had led to less violence in the classroom.

Kids at a New York school work to promote peace and stop school violence by training to become peer mediators.

Most students are antiviolence

In addition to parents and teachers taking a stance against violence, students are also concerned with stopping the violence. In fact, the majority of students are antiviolence. Only a small percentage of students actually commit the serious violent crimes at school. Most students want a peaceful school environment. A 1998 Harris poll found that nine out of ten teenagers said they would be willing to take an active role against violence in their schools.

Across the country, students are becoming involved in programs designed to make their schools safer. Peer mediation is one way students have actively worked to reduce school violence. Peer mediators usually work as a team of two to resolve a conflict between two other students who have agreed to accept the outside help. Peer mediators must remain neutral while they help the disputants look at the problem from different angles, recommend compromises, and try to come to a mutually agreeable, nonviolent solution. The peer mediator strategy is gaining in popularity in schools with conflict resolution programs and shows promise.

Students have also begun national efforts to stop violence in schools. After the Columbine rampage, students in Colorado started an organization called Sane Alternatives to the Firearms Epidemic (SAFE). The organization seeks to fix loopholes in gun control laws. "I believe that if students can organize, they can effect change,"[90] says Ben Gelt, one of the student founders of SAFE.

Perhaps the largest effect on school violence that students have had has been exposing plots for violence at their schools. In several cases, students have foiled plots of violence by reporting them to an adult. In St. Charles, Missouri, for example, three sixth graders planned a killing spree for the last day of school modeled on the Jonesboro attack. Worried students who had heard about the plan told their parents, who in turn reported the plot to police. "Because of the awareness of the issues there," says Ronald Stephens, executive director of the school violence center at Pepperdine University, "school and law enforcement officials were able to put a stop to a potentially deadly copycat incident."[91]

Schools and communities working together

The most successful violence prevention programs so far are those in which schools and communities work together. Each school offers a unique situation, and people closest to a particular school, whether educators, parents of students at the school, or members of the surrounding community, are in the best position to judge whether a specific violence prevention strategy fits their situation. "What works in Queens, [New York,] is often going to be a waste of resources in Oklahoma," says Richard Seder, director of education for the Reason Public Policy Institute, which conducted a comprehensive study of violence prevention strategies. "Policymakers should recognize the diversity of our schools, and rather than saddle school boards with restrictions and mandates, promote community-oriented innovation."[92]

Researchers and government agencies alike favor such an integrated approach. In its review of the $4 billion in government funds spent on programs for at-risk youths in 1996, the General Accounting Office could not determine whether violence prevention programs were effective. However, it did find that linking school-based programs to community groups showed promise.

Integrated programs between a school and community often provide classes and outreach projects that result in decreased school violence. The Fourth Street Elementary School in Athens, Georgia, is an example of collaboration between school and community. Health, welfare, government, and community agencies have teamed up with local businesses to provide family counseling services and classes for parents at the school.

Another integrated approach that is gaining in popularity is the full-service school. In California, these are called Second Shift Schools. Elsewhere, they are known as Beacon Centers, YouthNet Centers, New Beginnings, or Village Centers. These schools open their doors before and after school hours and offer programs that include athletics, drama and music classes, computer and job training, counseling, health clinics, social services, and leadership and volunteer groups. These centers allow young people to interact with healthy adult role models, afford them a sense of inclusiveness and value to the community, and often have a higher academic record.

After school is a vital time

After school is a vital time for schools and communities to provide positive outlets for youths since most juvenile crime occurs between 3:00 and 8:00 P.M. Yet more than one in four children and adolescents lack a safe haven after school, and researchers estimate that more than 2 million latchkey children go home alone every day. Ramon Cortines, chancellor of the Board of Education for New York City and also a consultant to the secretary of education, writes,

> Students who are productively occupied after school hours are much less likely to become involved in inappropriate

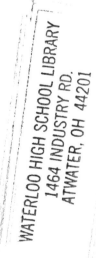

activities. By engaging in a positive outlet for their energies, they learn self-reliance and self-esteem, and many extracurricular activities afford the opportunity to learn discipline, leadership, and teamwork skills.[93]

Because so many people recognize the importance of constructive after-school activities, there are more than five hundred federally funded organizations and about the same number of privately funded organizations aimed at preventing youth violence by offering activities during non–school hours. Marcia Chaiken, a violence prevention researcher, claims that the most effective after-school programs are those that are well designed and offer a variety of age-graded programs based on an understanding of children's developmental skills. She describes a positive after-school program:

> Typically the noise level is high, with chattering children, and compared to school settings the multitude of activities may seem chaotic. But in separate corners or side rooms designated as "quiet areas," children work with adults on homework assignments, sit transfixed at a computer terminal, or are engrossed in a story being read to them. Occasionally a child sits disconsolately in a time-out area waiting out a penalty for breaking a rule, or a child may be off in an out-of-ear-shot corner discussing a problem or concern with a staff member.[94]

Well-designed after-school programs can become a positive institution in the community and a strong force to counter school violence. Several national organizations such as Boys and Girls Clubs of America, Boy Scouts of America, Girls Incorporated, Girl Scouts of the USA, the National Association of Police Athletic Leagues (PAL), the National 4-H Council, and the YMCA offer stable, long-term programs designed to reduce youth delinquency in urban areas.

Society's future is at stake

The problem of school violence is one that continues to have a tremendous impact on the United States. Some schools are plagued by everyday violence and a culture of fear, while others deal with mass shootings. Regardless, the greatest concern is that school violence prevents stu-

dents from receiving a quality education, putting every-one's future at risk. Futrell writes,

> Americans cannot afford to ignore or minimize the magnitude of violence in schools and the implications it has for the larger society. . . . In five to ten years these young men and women will become part of the adult population. They are the people who will be expected to safeguard and enhance the civil, human, political, and economic rights of the citizens of our country. It is the future of this nation and the kind of society we want that is at stake.[95]

The Girl Scouts is one of many organizations that now offers long-term programs designed to reduce youth delinquency in urban areas.

Notes

Introduction

1. Quoted in *Maclean's*, "Teens Under Siege," May 3, 1999, p. 22.

2. Quoted in *ABCnews*, "Kip Kinkel Gets Almost 112 Years," November 10, 1999. www.abcnews.go.com/sections/us/DailyNews/kinkel_sentencing991110.html.

Chapter 1: The Scope of School Violence

3. Quoted in Kathy Koch, "School Violence: Are American Schools Safe?" *CQ Researcher*, October 9, 1998, p. 883.

4. Quoted in Nancy Gibbs, "The Littleton Massacre," *Time*, May 3, 1999, p. 30.

5. Vincent Schiraldi "How Distorted Coverage of Juvenile Crime Affects Public Policy," Justice Policy Institute press release, November 11, 1999. www.cjcj.org.

6. Quoted in Sandra Arbetter, "Violence: A Growing Threat," *Current Health 2*, February 1995, p. 6.

7. Koch, "School Violence," p. 885.

8. Quoted in Koch, "School Violence," p. 883.

9. Margaret Hamburg, "Youth Violence Is a Public Health Concern," in Delbert S. Elliott, Beatrix A. Hamburg, and Kirk R. Williams, eds., *Violence in American Schools*. Cambridge, England: Cambridge University Press, 1998, p. 3.

10. National Center for Education Statistics, *Indicators of School Crime and Safety, 1999*. Washington, DC: U.S. Departments of Education and Justice, p. 6. www.ojp.usdoj.gov/bjs/.

11. Raymond Lorion, "Exposure to Urban Violence," in Elliott et al., *Violence in American Schools*, p. 297.

12. Quoted in Koch, "School Violence," p. 892.

Chapter 2: The Roots of School Violence

13. Charles Patrick Ewing, *Kids Who Kill*. Lexington, MA: Lexington Books, 1990, p. 8.

14. Quoted in Rolf Loeber and Magda Stouthamer-Loeber, "Juvenile Aggression at Home and at School," in Elliott et al., *Violence in American Schools*, p. 115.

15. Barbara Lerner, "The Killer Narcissists," *National Review*, May 17, 1999, p. 34.

16. Hamburg, "Youth Violence Is a Public Health Concern," p. 35.

17. Quoted in Melba Coleman, "Victims of Violence: Helping Kids Cope," in Allan M. Hoffman, ed., *Schools, Violence, and Society*. Westport, CT: Praeger, 1996, p. 201.

18. Larry J. Siegel and Joseph J. Senna, *Juvenile Delinquency: Theory, Practice, and Law*, 5th ed. St. Paul, MN: West Publishing, 1994, p. 145.

19. Lorion, "Exposure to Urban Violence," p. 306.

20. Quoted in Adam Cohen, "A Curse of Cliques," *Time*, May 3, 1999, p. 45.

21. Quoted in *Maclean's*, "Teens Under Siege," p. 22.

22. Quoted in Liz Stevens, "Nothing Funny About Teasing," *Knight-Ridder/Tribune News Service*, May 25, 1999, p. K6316.

23. Quoted in Koch, "School Violence," p. 886.

24. National Center for Education Statistics, *Indicators of School Crime and Safety, 1999*, p. 35.

25. Quoted in Keith Geiger, "NEA's Perspective and Policies on Violence in Schools," in Hoffman, ed., *Schools, Violence, and Society*, p. 227.

26. Kelly Patricia O'Meara, "Doping Kids," *Insight on the News*, June 28, 1999, p. 10.

27. Quoted in O'Meara, "Doping Kids," p. 10.

28. Quoted in O'Meara, "Doping Kids," p. 10.

Chapter 3: Violence in the Media

29. Daniel Derksen and Victor Strasburger, "Media and Television Violence: Effects on Violence, Aggression, and

Antisocial Behaviors in Children," in Hoffman, ed., *Schools, Violence, and Society*, p. 62.

30. Derksen and Strasburger, "Media and Television Violence," p. 63.

31. Derksen and Strasburger, "Media and Television Violence," p. 62.

32. Thomas Jipping, "Diagnosing the Cultural Virus," *World & I*, July 1999, p. 80.

33. Derksen and Strasburger, "Media and Television Violence," p. 64.

34. Quoted in Derksen and Strasburger, "Media and Television Violence," p. 65.

35. Derksen and Strasburger, "Media and Television Violence," p. 62.

36. Derksen and Strasburger, "Media and Television Violence," p. 70.

37. Quoted in Thomas L. Jipping, "Diagnosing the Cultural Virus," p. 80.

38. Quoted in Kathy Koch, "Society's Glorification of Violence," *CQ Researcher*, October 9, 1998, p. 888.

39. Quoted in Jipping, "Diagnosing the Cultural Virus," p. 80.

40. Jipping, "Diagnosing the Cultural Virus," p. 80.

41. Jipping, "Diagnosing the Cultural Virus," p. 80.

42. Quoted in Koch, "Society's Glorification of Violence," p. 888.

43. Quoted in Gayle Hanson, "The Violent World of Video Games," *Insight on the News*, June 28, 1999, p. 14.

44. Quoted in John Leo, "When Life Imitates Video," *U.S. News & World Report*, May 3, 1999, p. 14.

45. Quoted in Mark A. Kellner, "Taking on Tinseltown," *Christianity Today*, June 14, 1999, p. 16.

46. Leo, "When Life Imitates Video," p. 14.

47. Quoted in Alexandra Hanson-Harding, "Ending School Violence," *Junior Scholastic*, October 4, 1999, pp. 10+.

48. Quoted in Richard Corliss, "Bang, You're Dead," *Time*, May 3, 1999, p. 50.

Chapter 4: Gangs in Schools

49. William P. Evans, Carla Fitzgerald, Dan Weigel, and Sarah Chvilicek, "Are Rural Gang Members Similar to Their Urban Peers?" *Youth and Society*, March 1999, p. 268.

50. Shirley Lal, Dhyan Lal, and Charles Achilles, *Handbook on Gangs in Schools*. Thousand Oaks, CA: Corwin Press, 1993, p. 9.

51. Quoted in Coleman, "Victims of Violence," pp. 201–202.

52. Quoted in *Current Events*, "Armed and Dangerous: Life Inside Youth Gangs," January 24, 1994, p. 2A.

53. Lal et al., *Handbook on Gangs in Schools*, p. 32.

54. Quoted in Anita Merina, "Stopping Violence Starts with Students," *NEA Today*, February 1993, p. 4.

55. Tina Juarez, "Where Homeboys Feel at Home in School," *Educational Leadership*, February 1996, p. 30.

56. Quoted in Anita Merina, "Peacemaker," *NEA Today*, February 1996, p. 7.

57. Quoted in *Current Events*, "Armed and Dangerous," p. 2A.

58. Thomas Capozzoli and Steve McVey, *Kids Killing Kids: Managing Violence and Gangs in Schools*. Boca Raton, FL: St. Lucie Press, 2000, p. 81.

59. Lal et al., *Handbook on Gangs in Schools*, p. 29.

60. Capozzoli and McVey, *Kids Killing Kids*, p. 81.

61. Lal et al., *Handbook on Gangs in Schools*, p. 8.

62. Quoted in Thomas Toch and Marc Silver, "Violence in Schools," *U.S. News & World Report*, November 8, 1993, p. 30.

63. Frank Aquila and Douglas Clay, "Gangs and America's Schools," *Phi Delta Kappan*, September 1994, p. 65.

64. Aquila and Clay, "Gangs and America's Schools," p. 65.

Chapter 5: Guns in Schools

65. Quoted in Toch and Silver, "Violence in Schools," p. 34.

66. Quoted in Koch, "School Violence," p. 887.

67. Bill Smith and Sherry McMorris, "Would Stronger Gun Control Laws Make Schools Safer?" *NEA Today*, October 1999, p. 11.

68. Quoted in Koch, "School Violence," p. 886.

69. Ewing, *Kids Who Kill*, p. 122.

70. Quoted in Stephen Braun, "Tough Gun Bill Gains in Maryland," *Los Angeles Times*, April 1, 2000, p. A9.

71. Quoted in Koch, "School Violence," p. 887.

72. Quoted in Koch, "School Violence," p. 887.

73. Don Feder, "Arkansas Violence: Blaming Guns Is Easy," *Human Events*, April 24, 1998, p. 9.

74. Quoted in Koch, "School Violence," p. 887.

75. Toch and Silver, "Violence in Schools," p. 32.

76. Quoted in Koch, "School Violence," p. 885.

77. Quoted in Jonathan Alter, "Moving Beyond the Blame Game," *Newsweek*, May 17, 1999, p. 30.

Chapter 6: Making Schools Safe

78. Deborah Prothrow-Stith and Sher Quaday, "Communities, Schools, and Violence," in Hoffman, ed., *Schools, Violence, and Society*, p. 158.

79. Quoted in *Current Health 2*, "When Violence Comes to School," April/May 1998 p. 6.

80. Quoted in Karen Gutloff, "Anger in the Halls," *NEA Today*, October 1999, p. 8.

81. *Economist*, "A Bullet for Teacher," July 24, 1993, p. A26.

82. Quoted in Mary Lord, "The Violent-Kid Profile," *U.S. News & World Report*, October 11, 1999, p. 56.

83. Quoted in Koch, "School Violence," p. 885.

84. Quoted in Kathy Koch, "Safe Schools Hotline to the Rescue," *CQ Researcher*, October 9, 1998, p. 895.

85. Quoted in Koch, "School Violence," p. 886.

86. Quoted in Lord, "The Violent-Kid Profile," p. 56.

87. Mary Futrell, "Violence in the Classroom: A Teacher's Perspective," in Hoffman, ed., *Schools, Violence, and Society*, p. 16.

88. Quoted in Futrell, "Violence in the Classroom," p. 3.

89. Futrell, "Violence in the Classroom," pp. 14, 17.

90. Quoted in Hanson-Harding, "Ending School Violence," p. 12.

91. Quoted in Cheryl Wetzstein, "Make Aware, or Scare?" *Insight on the News*, July 6, 1998, p. 37.

92. Quoted in Koch, "School Violence," p. 896.

93. Ramon Cortines, "The New York City Board of Education and Violence Prevention," in Hoffman, ed., *Schools, Violence, and Society*, p. 271.

94. Marcia Chaiken, "Tailoring Established After-School Programs to Meet Urban Realities," in Elliott, *Violence in American Schools*, p. 358.

95. Futrell, "Violence in the Classroom," p. 17.

Glossary

assault: The threat of causing harm through physical contact.

battery: The actual physical injury of one person by another with the intention to do harm.

bullying: A continued pattern of harassment by one individual against another who is relatively helpless; the harassment can be physical, verbal, or psychological.

community: A specific group of individuals who share certain values and commitments to each other and who organize their individual behaviors at least partly in response to the larger group's values.

firearm: A rifle or pistol.

gang: A group of young people who have been involved in enough antisocial activity to gain the attention of the criminal justice system.

homicide: The killing of one human being by another.

interpersonal violence: Violence between two people, including murder, rape, assault, robbery, and arson.

juvenile: A young person.

learned behavior: Early learning experiences within the family that provide the foundation for later behavior.

narcissism: Excessive feelings of self-love.

psychological profiling: A technique that uses potential signs to identify troubled persons before they commit an act of violence.

psychotropic drugs: Mind-altering drugs designed to affect personality, behavior, and mood; the most common examples are Luvox, Prozac, and Ritalin.

risk factor: An element of a person's life associated with a particular behavior such as violence.

sanctuary: A place set aside from larger societal concerns and traumas.

Organizations
to Contact

The following organizations work in some area that concerns school violence or its prevention. All offer publications and information to anyone interested in knowing more about the issue of school violence.

American Academy of Pediatrics,
Committee on Public Education
141 Northwest Point Blvd.
Elk Grove Village, IL 60007-1098
(847) 228-5005
fax: (847) 228-5097
Internet: www.aap.org

The AAP is committed to the overall physical, mental, and social health of children and adolescents. The Committee on Public Education has informative policy statements on the potentially harmful effects of the media on young people.

Center to Prevent Handgun Violence
1225 Eye St. NW, Suite 1100
Washington, DC 20005
(202) 898-0792
fax: (202) 371-9615
Internet: www.handguncontrol.org

The outreach arm of the nonprofit Handgun Control Inc., the center offers resources to educate the general public about the issues surrounding gun violence in the United States. The center works to reform the gun manufacturing industry and has several regional offices.

Educators for Social Responsibility
23 Garden St.
Cambridge, MA 02138
(800) 370-2515
Internet: http://euphoria.benjerry.com/esr/

ESR coordinates the national dissemination of the Resolving Conflict Creatively Program (RCCP) through the RCCP National Center. RCCP is a comprehensive, K–12 school-based program in conflict resolution and intergroup relations that provides a model for preventing violence and creating caring learning communities. It is now the largest program of its kind in the country.

Justice Policy Institute
2208 Martin Luther King Jr. Ave. SE
Washington, DC 20020
(202) 678-9282
fax: (202) 678-9321
Internet: www.cjcj.org

A project of the private, nonprofit Center on Juvenile and Criminal Justice, this policy research group aims to reduce society's reliance on the use of incarceration as a solution to social problems.

National Coalition on Television Violence
5132 Newport Ave.
Bethesda, MD 20816
(301) 986-0362
fax: (301) 656-7031
Internet: www.nctvv.org

NCTV is an educational and research organization that works to decrease the amount of violence on TV, in the movies, and in other forms of the media. It sponsors seminars and publishes educational materials.

National Conference for Community and Justice
475 Park Ave. S, 19th Floor
New York, NY 10016-6901
Internet: www.nccj.org

The National Conference for Community and Justice, (NCCJ) founded in 1927 as the National Conference of Christians and Jews, is a human relations organization dedicated to fighting bias, bigotry, and racism in America. NCCJ promotes understanding and respect among all races, religions, and cultures through advocacy, conflict resolution, and education.

National Education Association
1201 16th St. NW
Washington, DC 20036
(202) 833-4000
fax on demand: (888) 2GETNEA
Internet: www.nea.org

America's oldest and largest organization dedicated to advancing the cause of public education, the NEA claims more than 2.3 million members. It works at the local, state, national, and international levels to improve public education.

National Institute on Media and the Family
606 24th Ave. S, Suite 606
Minneapolis, MN 55454
(616) 672-5437 or (888) 672-5437
Internet: www.mediaandthefamily.org

As a national resource center, the institute offers resources about the impact of the media on children and families. The institute's website evaluates and rates the content of movies, TV shows, and computer games from a family-friendly perspective.

National Rifle Association
Institute for Legislative Action
1600 Rhode Island Ave. NW
Washington, DC 20036
(202) 828-6330 or (800) NRA-3888
Internet: www.nra.org

The NRA is an organization of target shooters, hunters, gun collectors, and others interested in firearms and gun advocacy. It has lobbied against gun control laws and has many programs on gun safety training.

National School Boards Association
1680 Duke St.
Alexandria, VA 22314
(703) 838-6722
fax: (703) 683-7590
Internet: www.nsba.org

An association of state school boards, the NSBA provides resources to involve school boards in discussing and implementing changes that will improve student achievement. It also monitors legislation and regulations that affect the funding and quality of public schools.

National School Safety Center
141 Duesenberg Dr., Suite 11
Westlake Village, CA 91362
(805) 373-9977
fax: (805) 373-9277
Internet: www.nssc1.org

Created in 1984 by presidential directive, this nonprofit organization has a wealth of resources on school safety, training, and prevention. The NSSC also identifies strategies and promising programs that support safe schools for children worldwide.

National Urban League
120 Wall St.
New York, NY 10005
(212) 558-5300

Founded in 1910, the National Urban League is a nonprofit, community-based social and civil rights organization. Its mission is to assist African Americans in the achievement of social and economic equality and encourages the African American community to rely on its own strengths and resources to find solutions to its problems.

**Office of Juvenile Justice and
Delinquency Prevention, Justice Department**
810 Seventh St. NW,
8th Floor

Washington, DC 20531
(202) 307-5911
fax: (202) 307-2093
Internet: www.ncjrs.org/ojjhome.htm

The OJJDP administers most federal programs aimed at delinquency prevention and treatment. It maintains a broad database of up-to-date information on all aspects of school violence.

Students Against Violence Everywhere (SAVE)
c/o Mothers Against Violence
105 14th Ave., Suite 2-A
Seattle, WA 98122
(206) 323-2303 or (800) 897-7697
fax: (206) 323-2132
Internet: www.mavia.org/save.htm

SAVE is a program open to all students who want to change attitudes and behaviors that contribute to violence. SAVE empowers students to create their own solutions and strategies for safer schools and communities through student-led projects to address issues of violence they think are important in their communities and schools.

Suggestions for Further Reading

Nancy Day, *Violence in Schools: Learning in Fear.* Springfield, NJ: Enslow, 1996. A broad look at the causes of school violence. The book also suggests what students can do to make schools safe as well as protect themselves from violence.

Patricia Occhiuzzo Giggans and Barrie Levy, *50 Ways to a Safer World: Everyday Actions You Can Take to Prevent Violence in Neighborhoods, Schools, and Communities.* Seattle: Seal Press, 1997. A book of ideas and suggestions for making your community and school safer. Though aimed mostly at adults, it has helpful suggestions for reviewing a school's safety levels and for how to be street smart.

Henry H. Kim, ed., *Guns and Violence.* San Diego: Greenhaven Press, 1999. A readable collection of articles that presents all sides of the gun control debate.

Anna Kreiner, *Everything You Need to Know About School Violence.* New York: Rosen, 1996. Most notable for a chapter on preventing school violence with suggestions for what students can do about the problem.

Maryann Miller, *Coping with Weapons and Violence in Your School and on Your Streets.* New York: Rosen, 1993. Filled with anecdotes, this book explores the causes and effects of violence. It also has suggestions for practicing conflict resolution and how to join the fight against violence.

David E. Newton, *Gun Control: An Issue for the Nineties.* Hillside, NJ: Enslow, 1992. This book presents arguments for and against gun control.

Janelle Rohr, ed., *Violence in America: Opposing Viewpoints*. San Diego: Greenhaven Press, 1990. A collection of opinions from magazines, journals, books, and newspapers written by a wide range of individuals. The book presents a balance of opinions on each individual topic and emphasizes analyzing each writer's type of argument.

Jay Schleifer, *Everything You Need to Know About Weapons in School and at Home*. New York: Rosen, 1994. Inspired by his daughter's experience with a school shooting, the author gives a brief history of gun laws in the United States and suggests why youths bring weapons to school.

Works Consulted

Books

Theresa M. Bey and Gwendolyn Y. Turner, *Making School a Place of Peace*. Thousand Oaks, CA: Corwin Press, 1996. A book with strategies for creating a peaceful school environment.

Thomas Capozzoli and Steve McVey, *Kids Killing Kids: Managing Violence and Gangs in Schools*. Boca Raton, FL: St. Lucie Press, 2000. A handbook that describes several of the high-profile school shootings and presents methods that parents and educators can use to prevent and reduce school violence.

Rose Duhon-Sells, ed., *Dealing with Youth Violence: What Schools and Communities Need to Know*. Bloomington, IN: National Educational Service, 1995. A compilation of writings that explores the causes and possible solutions to school violence.

Delbert S. Elliott, Beatrix A. Hamburg, and Kirk R. Williams, eds., *Violence in American Schools*. Cambridge, England: Cambridge University Press, 1998. A scholarly view of school violence from established authors in several fields.

Charles Patrick Ewing, *Kids Who Kill*. Lexington, MA: Lexington Books, 1990. The author includes numerous anecdotes in his exploration of several aspects of juvenile homicide.

James Garbarino, Nancy Dubrow, Kathleen Kostelny, and Carole Pardo, *Children in Danger*. San Francisco: Jossey Bass, 1992. In conjunction with the Erikson Institute for

Advanced Study in Child Development, this book is written to help professionals who work with children in violent communities understand what it is like to be a child in an urban war zone.

Todd Ian Herrenkohl, *An Examination of Neighborhood Context and Risk for Youth Violence.* Ph.D. dissertation, University of Washington, 1998. A statistical and theoretical analysis of the 1990 census for Seattle. The results suggest that youths' levels of attachment to their neighborhoods are related to community stability and neighborhood disadvantage.

Marie Somers Hill and Frank W. Hill, *Creating Safe Schools: What Principals Can Do.* Thousand Oaks, CA: Corwin Press, 1994. A handbook to help school principals achieve effective communities of learners.

Allan M. Hoffman, ed., *Schools, Violence, and Society.* Westport, CT: Praeger, 1996. A multifaceted look at school violence with writings by scholars and educators.

David W. Johnson and Roger T. Johnson, *Reducing School Violence Through Conflict Resolution.* Alexandria, VA: Association for Supervision and Curriculum Development, 1995. Discusses how schools can create a cooperative learning environment.

Shirley Lal, Dhyan Lal, and Charles Achilles, *Handbook on Gangs in Schools.* Thousand Oaks, CA: Corwin Press, 1993. An overview of what gangs do and who gang members are. It suggests strategies for reducing gang-related activities at school and in communities.

Linda Lantieri and Janet Patti, *Waging Peace in Our Schools.* Boston: Beacon Press, 1996. Closely tied to their work in the Resolving Conflict Creatively Program, the authors provide advice on implementing conflict resolution programs at home and at school.

Carol Silverman Saunders, *Safe at School: Awareness and Action for Parents of Kids Grades K–12.* Minneapolis, MN:

Free Spirit Publishing, 1994. Along with statistics on school violence, this book provides action plans for parents who desire to make schools safer.

Larry J. Siegel and Joseph J. Senna, *Juvenile Delinquency: Theory, Practice, and Law*. 5th ed. St. Paul, MN: West Publishing, 1994. This graduate-level textbook explores all aspects of the issue of juvenile delinquency.

Meredith W. Watts, ed., *Cross-Cultural Perspectives on Youth and Violence*. Stamford, CT: JAI Press, 1998. A multinational examination of violence and bullying in other cultures.

Franklin E. Zimring, *American Youth Violence.* New York: Oxford University Press, 1998. Provides a comprehensive, unique look at youth violence. The author debunks the idea of a future wave of youth violence in America and suggests several changes for the juvenile justice system.

Maxine Baca Zinn and D. Stanley Eitzen, *Diversity in Families*. 4th ed. New York: HarperCollins College, 1996. This college-level textbook explores the modern family against larger social influences.

Periodicals

Jonathan Alter, "Moving Beyond the Blame Game," *Newsweek*, May 17, 1999.

Nick Anderson, "Assault on Violence: As Twin Anniversaries Approach, Nation Wrestles with Gun Control, Terrorism," *Seattle Times*, April 12, 2000.

Frank Aquila and Douglas Clay, "Gangs and America's Schools," *Phi Delta Kappan*, September 1994.

Sandra Arbetter, "Violence: A Growing Threat," *Current Health 2*, February 1995.

Randolph C. Arndt, "School Violence in America's Cities," research report of the National League of Cities, November 1994.

Shay Bilchik, "Juvenile Justice Bulletin," Office of Juvenile Justice and Delinquency Prevention, May 1998.

——, "1996 National Youth Gang Survey," Office of Juvenile Justice and Delinquency Prevention, July 1999.

Cornelia Blanchette, "At-Risk and Delinquent Youth: Multiple Programs Lack Coordinated Federal Effort," General Accounting Office, November 1997.

Jonah Blank and Warren Cohen, "Prayer Circle Murders," *U.S. News & World Report*, December 15, 1997.

Evelyn Brady, "How to Survive Urban Violence with Hope," *English Journal*, September 1995.

Stephen Braun, "Tough Gun Bill Gains in Maryland," *Los Angeles Times*, April 1, 2000.

Allen Carey-Webb, "Youth Violence and the Language Arts," *English Journal*, September 1995.

Gail Russell Chaddock, "Act of Valor May Help Georgia Town to Heal," *Christian Science Monitor*, May 24, 1999.

Peter G. Chronis, "Litigation Against Shooters, Gun Makers Supported," *Denver Post*, November 26, 1999.

——, "Shootings Bring Sadness, Then Lawsuits," *Denver Post*, November 26, 1999.

Adam Cohen, "Criminals as Copycats," *Time*, May 31, 1999.

——, "A Curse of Cliques," *Time*, May 3, 1999.

Charles Colson and Nancy Pearcey, "How Evil Became Cool," *Christianity Today*, August 9, 1999.

Richard Corliss, "Bang, You're Dead," *Time*, May 3, 1999.

Current Events, "Armed and Dangerous: Life Inside Youth Gangs," January 24, 1994.

Current Health 2, "When Violence Comes to School," April/May 1998.

Robert H. DuRant, Frank Treiber, Elizabeth Goodman, and Elizabeth R. Woods, "Intentions to Use Violence Among Young Adolescents," *Pediatrics*, December 1996.

Economist, "A Bullet for Teacher," July 24, 1993.

William P. Evans, Carla Fitzgerald, Dan Weigel, and Sarah Chvilicek, "Are Rural Gang Members Similar to Their Urban Peers?" *Youth and Society*, March 1999.

Don Feder, "Arkansas Violence: Blaming Guns Is Easy," *Human Events*, April 24, 1998.

Kevin M. Fitzpatrick, "Violent Victimization Among America's School Children," *Journal of Interpersonal Violence*, October 1999.

Erika Fortgang, "How They Got the Guns," *Rolling Stone*, June 10, 1999.

William A. Galston, "A Look at Reacting to Violence; Activism Has Its Limits," *Washington Post*, May 23, 1999.

John Garvey, "Jonesboro, Arkansas," *Commonweal*, April 24, 1998.

Joan Gaustad, "Schools Respond to Gangs and Violence," Oregon School Study Council, May 1991.

Ted Gest, "Quelling Teen Crime with Tough Love," *U.S. News & World Report*, October 19, 1998.

Nancy Gibbs, "The Littleton Massacre," *Time*, May 3, 1999.

Nancy Gibbs and Timothy Roche, "The Columbine Tapes," *Time*, December 20, 1999.

Randi Goldberg, "Boy, 6, Shoots, Kills Girl in Class," *San Diego Union-Tribune*, March 1, 2000.

William Greider, "Will the Smart Gun Save Lives?" *Rolling Stone*, August 6, 1998.

Dave Grossman, "We Are Training Our Kids to Kill," *Saturday Evening Post*, September 1999.

Karen Gutloff, "Anger in the Halls," *NEA Today*, October 1999.

Gayle Hanson, "The Violent World of Video Games," *Insight on the News*, June 28, 1999.

Alexandra Hanson-Harding, "Ending School Violence," *Junior Scholastic*, October 4, 1999.

Jim Henderson, "Halloween Essay Lands 13-Year-Old Behind Bars," *Houston Chronicle*, November 4, 1999.

Michael deCourcy Hinds, "Gun-Weary Americans Applaud Controls," *American Demographics*, April 2000.

Michael Janofsky, "A Columbine Student Is Seized in a Threat to 'Finish the Job,'" *New York Times*, October 22, 1999.

Thomas L. Jipping, "Diagnosing the Cultural Virus," *World & I*, July 1999.

Tamara Jones, "Look Back in Sorrow," *Good Housekeeping*, November 1998.

Tina Juarez, "Where Homeboys Feel at Home in School," *Educational Leadership*, February 1996.

Wendy Kaminer, "Second Thoughts on the Second Amendment," *Atlantic Monthly*, March, 1996.

Mark A. Kellner, "Taking on Tinseltown," *Christianity Today*, June 14, 1999.

Kathy Koch, "Safe Schools Hotline to the Rescue," *CQ Researcher*, October 9, 1998.

Kathy Koch, "School Violence: Are American Schools Safe?" *CQ Researcher*, October 9, 1998.

Kathy Koch, "Society's Glorification of Violence," *CQ Researcher*, October 9, 1998.

John Leo, "When Life Imitates Video," *U.S. News & World Report*, May 3, 1999.

Barbara Lerner, "The Killer Narcissists," *National Review*, May 17, 1999.

Mary Lord, "The Violent-Kid Profile," *U.S. News & World Report*, October 11, 1999.

John R. Lott Jr., "More Guns, Less Violent Crime," *Wall Street Journal*, August 28, 1996.

Maclean's, "Teens Under Siege," May 3, 1999.

Timothy W. Maier and Michael Rust, "A Decline in Crime?" *Insight on the News*, April 27, 1998.

Anita Merina, "Peacemaker," *NEA Today*, February 1996.

———, "Stopping Violence Starts with Students," *NEA Today*, February 1993.

Nikki L. Murdick and Barbara C. Gartin, "How to Handle Students Exhibiting Violent Behaviors," *Clearing House*, May/June 1993.

NEA Today, "Meet Janet Reno," November 1997.

Sasha Nemecek, "Forestalling Violence," *Scientific American*, September 1998.

New York Times, "New Curriculum Sought to Curb Student Violence," October 8, 1999.

New York Times Upfront, "Getting a Handle on Guns," September 6, 1999.

Newsweek, "The Killing Season," June 1, 1998.

Kelly Patricia O'Meara, "Doping Kids," *Insight on the News*, June 28, 1999.

Randy M. Page and Jon Hammermeister, "Weapon-Carrying and Youth Violence," *Adolescence*, Fall 1997.

Sherry Parmet and Jill Spielvogel, "Crime Is Up but Schools Still Safe, Report Says," *San Diego Union-Tribune*, March 1, 2000.

People Weekly, "Roll Call of the Dead," June 14, 1993.

Susan Reed, "Reading, Writing, and Murder: A Survey of Death in America's Public Schools Shows There's No Sanctuary from the Culture of Violence," *People Weekly*, June 14, 1993.

Patrick Rogers, "Mortal Lessons," *People Weekly*, June 8, 1998.

Vincent Schiraldi, "Making Sense of Juvenile Homicides in America," *America*, July 17, 1999.

Seattle Post-Intelligencer, "US House Offers Weak Measure on Gun Control," April 16, 2000.

Seattle Times, "Daily Briefing," June 23, 1999.

——, "Suit Filed in School Shooting," July 3, 1999.

Danielle Sewell, "Media Plays Big Role," *Seattle Times*, November 20, 1999.

Beth Shuster, "Living in Fear," *Los Angeles Times*, August 23, 1998.

Michael D. Simpson, "Who Can Sue? For What?" *NEA Today*, April 1993.

Bill Smith and Sherry McMorris, "Would Stronger Gun Control Laws Make Schools Safer?" *NEA Today*, October 1999.

Shelley Smith, "A Victory for Fear," *Sports Illustrated*, November 11, 1991.

Liz Stevens, "Nothing Funny About Teasing," *Knight-Ridder/Tribune News Service*, May 25, 1999.

Thomas Toch and Marc Silver, "Violence in Schools," *U.S. News & World Report*, November 8, 1993.

Sheila Weller, "Girls in the Gang: A Nineties Nightmare," *Cosmopolitan*, August 1994.

Cheryl Wetzstein, "Make Aware, or Scare?" *Insight on the News*, July 6, 1998.

Internet Sources

ABCnews, "Clinton Pushes for More Restrictions," May 21, 1999. www.abcnews.go.com/sections/us/DailyNews/guncontrol990521.html.

——, "Kip Kinkel Gets Almost 112 Years," November 10, 1999. www.abcnews.go.com/sections/us/DailyNews/kinkel_sentencing991110.html.

———, "Prior Threats? Angry at Mom's Death, Boy Allegedly Talked of 'Blasting School,'" November 21, 1999. www.abcnews.go.com/sections/us/DailyNews/shooting991121.html.

———, "Recording Infamy? Police Say Columbine Shooters Made Videotapes for Police," November 11, 1999. www.abcnews.go.com/sections/us/DailyNews/columbine991111.html.

Jeff Barnard, "Sentencing Nears for Kip Kinkel," November 10, 1999. www.abcnews.go.com/sections/us/DailyNews/kinkel991110.html.

Elizabeth Donohue, Vincent Schiraldi, and Jason Ziedenberg, "School House Hype: School Shootings and the Real Risks Kids Face in America," July 29, 1998. www.cjcj.org.

National Center for Education Statistics, *Indicators of School Crime and Safety, 1999*. Washington, DC: U.S. Departments of Education and Justice. www.ojp.usdoj.gov/bjs/.

Herb J. O'Connor, "The Cleavers Don't Live Here Anymore," *ABCnews*, May 20, 1999. www.abcnews.go.com/sections/living/DailyNews/nightline_teenviolence990520.html.

Vincent Schiraldi, "How Distorted Coverage of Juvenile Crime Affects Public Policy," Justice Policy Institute press release, November 22, 1999. www.cjcj.org.

Robert Weller, "Columbine Guilty Plea: Man Admits Selling Weapons to Columbine Gunmen," *ABCnews*, August 18, 1999. www.abcnews.go.com/sections/us/DailyNews/columbine990818.html.

White House, "Vice President Al Gore Announces New Information Finding Juvenile Violent Crime and Victimization Highest During After School Hours," September 17, 1999. www.ojjdp.ncjrs.org/about/press/ojp990917.html.

Index

Picture Credits

Cover: © Reuters NewMedia Inc./CORBIS
© AFP/CORBIS, 63
© Nubar Alexanian/CORBIS, 20
© Philip James Corwin/CORBIS, 27
© 1993 Jerome Friar/Impact Visuals, 61
© Carolina Kroon/Impact Visuals, 67, 77
© Daniel Laine/CORBIS, 18, 53
© 1997 Alain McLaughlin/Impact Visuals, 71
© 1994 Alain McLaughlin/Impact Visuals, 51
PhotoDisc, 23, 25, 28, 33, 36, 69
© 1997 Rick Reinhard/Impact Visuals, 73
© 1993 Rick Reinhard/Impact Visuals, 75
© 1997 Richard Renaldi/Impact Visuals, 49
Reuters/Gary Caskey/Archive Photos, 7, 10
Reuters/Ho/Archive Photos, 30
Reuters/Chris Martinez/Archive Photos, 41
Reuters/Fred Prouser/Archive Photos, 65
Reuters/Mike Segar/Archive Photos, 81
Reuters/John Sommers II/Archive Photos, 39
Martha Schierholz, 12, 13, 46
© Jim Tynan/Impact Visuals, 52

About the Author

Jeff P. Jones graduated from the University of Colorado at Denver in 1995. He also attended the University of Washington, where he received an MA in International Studies in 1997. He is a freelance writer and lives in Seattle, Washington.